BOOK OF THE DESCENDANTS OF
DOCTOR BENJAMIN LEE
and
DOROTHY GORDON

DOROTHY GORDON   (1880–1955)   c. 1902

BENJAMIN LEE GORDON, M.D. (1870–1965) c. 1916

CONTRIBUTORS

Gordon Philo Baker, M.D.

Jonathan Benjamin Baker, A.B., LL.B.

Benjamin Lee Gordon, II, A.B., M.A., Ph.D., M.D.

Cyrus Herzl Gordon, A.B., M.A., Ph.D.

Deborah Joanna Gordon, A.B.

Maurice Bear Gordon, A.B., M.D.

Rachel Kendall Gordon

Richard Frederick Gordon, M.D.

Sarah Yael Gordon

Susan Joan Gordon, M.D.

BOOK OF THE DESCENDANTS OF

Doctor Benjamin Lee
and
Dorothy Gordon

VENTNOR PUBLISHERS
VENTNOR, NEW JERSEY

Library of Congress Catalog Number: 73-169910
International Standard Book Number: 0-911566-11

Jonah's office, which consisted of one large room, looked more like a House of Study than a medical office. There were no surgical instruments in view and no drugs or apothecary's equipment. The walls were concealed by several large bookcases in which, in addition to Hebrew books, a large collection of old Hebrew newspapers were stored. Jonah could always be found studying the Talmud. He was greatly interested in Talmudic medicine, and strived at times to follow Talmudic medical practice. He occasionally resorted to spiritual healing. Thus, when applying a mustard plaster, he saw to it that the paper on which the mustard was spread was on a page from the Holy Scriptures or the Prayer Book. As such holy pages were not always available (for it was considered a sin to throw them away), he at times stealthily entered the anteroom of the synagogue (where the decayed Holy Books were deposited in large containers to be eventually taken with solemn ceremonies to the cemetery for burial) to renew his supply.

Benjamin Lee Gordon, M.D.: Between Two Worlds, New York, 1952, p. 20.

This book is affectionately dedicated to the following descendants of Doctor Benjamin Lee and Dorothy Gordon who were too young to contribute to this volume:

BRETT GORDON BAKER

GREGORY LAURENT BAKER

SETH EDWARD BAKER

CYRUS HERZL GORDON, II

DAN KENDALL GORDON

MAURICE BEAR GORDON, II

NOAH DANIEL GORDON

SORAYAWATI GORDON

Preface

Mrs. Dorothy Gordon, the matriarch of our family, died in 1955 at the age of 75. Doctor Benjamin Lee Gordon, our patriarch, died in 1965 at the age of 94. Long prior to their passing, it became apparent that these persons bequeathed to their children and grandchildren a special set of genetic and environmental values which profoundly affected all of their lives. During an age when the importance of worldly goods in attaining the good life has been substantially overemphasized, the descendants of the Gordons have remained relatively unaffected by such mundane values—even unto the fourth generation.

Mother's contribution to her progeny emphasized the importance of maternal love, personal integrity, self-sacrifice and philanthropy and her esteem of *quality* in both people and inanimate objects led to a deep appreciation of the finest of humanity and the arts. Father's stressed love of scholarship in its broadest sense with special emphasis on science and especially the value of the written word in the form of original texts in interpreting history. Both parents at all times exhibited undying loyalty to their descendants.

The present volume seeks to honor the memory of the Gordons in terms of their unusual bequest to their progeny and at the same time it serves to delineate the nature of their bequest via a group of articles written by their descendants.

The contributing authors of this volume include the following:

Cyrus Herzl Gordon, A.B., M.A., Ph.D., is Joseph Foster Professor of Near Eastern Studies and Chairman of the Department of Mediterranean Studies at Brandeis University. His most recent books include "Before Columbus," "Forgotten Scripts," "Ugaritic Textbook" and "Evidence for the Minoan Language."

Gordon Philo Baker, M.D., is an Allergist practicing in Seattle, Washington. He is a member of the faculty of the Medical School of the University of Washington.

Jonathan Benjamin Baker, A.B., LL.B., is a social planner in The Department of Social Planning and Community Development in Vancouver, B.C., Canada and the Director of The Community Music School of Greater Vancouver.

Benjamin Lee Gordon, II, A.B., M.A., Ph.D., M.D., is author of "Dyscrasias of Immunoglobulin Production: Their Impact on Modern Immunology" and senior author of "Essentials of Immunology."

Susan Joan Gordon, M.D., is a gastroenterologist and member of the faculty of The Jefferson Medical College. She is the author of a book of poems, "The Road I Travel."

Richard Frederick Gordon, M.D., is a Fellow in Cardiology at the Hahnemann Medical College and Hospital.

Deborah Joanna Gordon, A.B., is a graduate student at the University of Chicago.

Sarah Yael Gordon is an undergraduate student in Theater Arts at Brandeis University and as a junior has just been elected to Phi Beta Kappa.

Rachel Kendall Gordon is an undergraduate student at Brandeis University.

The undersigned practices Internal Medicine in Ventnor, New Jersey and is the author of "Aesculapius Comes to the Colonies: The Story of the Early Days of Medicine in the Thirteen Original Colonies."

Maurice Bear Gordon, M.D.

Contents

Illustrations

THE
SCIENCES

With the dissolution of the Jewish state, great changes took place in the cultural aspects of the Hebrews. The captivity in Babylon brought the exiles into contact with a new sphere of thought which had a wholesome influence on them, so that when they returned after seventy years to their homeland, they brought with them, in addition to their own intellectual store, also the new culture. They became known as "The People of the Book." Their teachers were known as *Soferim* (Scribes) because they occupied themselves in transcribing books, *Maskilim* (Enlightened Ones) and *Mevinim* (Men of Understanding). Daniel extolled scholarship: "They that be wise shall shine as the brightness of the firmament." A man of knowledge was considered greater than a prophet. Schools and academies were established all over Palestine. When Palestine came under the political supremacy of Greece, the Hellenic culture also exercised a great influence upon the Judeans. Thus the prophecy of Isaiah, that "the earth shall be full of the knowledge of the Lord as the waters cover the sea," was at last realized.

Benjamin Lee Gordon, M.D.: Medicine Among the Ancient Hebrews. Third Series *Annals of Medical History*, Vol. IV, No. 3, 1942, pp. 220–221.

CHAPTER 1

The Bat Creek Inscription

by

CYRUS H. GORDON, A.B., M.A., Ph.D.*

Roman contact with America around 200 A.D. has been established by the excavation of a sculptured clay head by archeologists at the pyramid of Calixtlahuaca in Mexico.[1] That there is no mistaking the facts or their implications has been demonstrated by Robert Heine-Geldern, "Ein römischer Fund aus dem vorkolumbischen Mexico," *Anzeiger der Oesterreichischen Akademie der Wissenschaften, Philosophische-historische Klasse* 98, 1961, pp. 117–119. This piece of solid evidence lends credence to previous accidental finds such as the Roman coins, bearing Latin inscriptions, found in the American Southeast since over a century and a half ago, as documented by John Haywood, *Natural and Aboriginal History of Tennessee*, George Wilson, Nashville, Tennessee, 1823 (republished by Mary U. Rothrock, McCowat-Mercer Press, Jackson, Tennessee, 1959). Haywood, the Chief Justice of the Supreme Court of Tennessee, was fortunately endowed with a judge's acumen in weighing evidence. Among the inscribed Roman coins he identified were one of the Antonines,[2] and another of Commodus.[3] Other coins pointing to contacts with the Roman Mediterranean during the second century A.D. have meanwhile come to light in the neighboring state of Kentucky, where inscribed Hebrew coins of Bar Kokhba's rebellion against Rome (132–135

---

*Joseph Foster Professor of Near Eastern Studies and Chairman of the Department of Mediterranean Studies at Brandeis University.

A.D.) were dug up in Louisville, Hopkinsville and Clay City. The coins are assorted (not duplicates of each other) and were found at different times in widely separated areas: at Louisville in 1932, Clay City in 1952, and Hopkinsville in 1967. These coins have been examined and identified by Professor Israel T. Naamani of the University of Louisville (*The Courier-Journal*, Louisville, of 12 July 1953, 14 March 1967, 20 March 1967).[4] Clay City (population under 500) had no citizens previously interested in—or even aware of—curiosa such as Bar Kokhba numismatics. The coin found there was sent to the late Professor Ralph Marcus of the University of Chicago who had no trouble in reading "Simon" (Bar Kokhba's personal name) on one side, and "Year 2 of the Freedom of Israel" (i.e., 133 A.D.) on the other. The Hebrew script is quite familiar from Jewish coins of the Roman period down to 135 A.D.; see Theodore Reinach, *Jewish Coins*, Argonaut, Chicago, 1966; Ya'akov Meshorer, *Jewish Coins of the Second Temple Period*, Am Hassefer, Tel-Aviv, 1967; Sylvia Haffner, *The History of Modern Israel's Money 1917–1967*, San Diego, California, 1967 (with good reproductions of ancient coins along with the modern coins they inspired).

It is against the background of the foregoing material that we must approach the excavation of a Hebrew inscription in a tomb at Bat Creek, Loudon County, in Eastern Tennessee. In the late 1880's an expedition of the Smithsonian Institution dug an unrifled tomb with nine skeletons. A tree atop the burial mound had sent its roots down among the bones at the bottom, and had died before the archeologists got there. Unfortunately the field notes do not tell us what kind of tree it was—nor even whether it was a hard or soft wood. Yet the dead tree suggests that the burial antedates the decipherment of the Old Hebrew (Canaanite) script by Gesenius early in the nineteenth century; and it certainly antedates the pioneer work on Hebrew coins (M. A. Levy, *Geschichte der jüdischen Münzen*, Nies'sche Buchdruckerei, Leipzig, 1862) with the first study of the coin script whose letter forms (pp. 136–137) happen to be those in closest agreement with the Bat Creek text.

The excavation and the objects found are described as follows by Cyrus Thomas (*Twelfth Annual Report of the Bureau of Ethnology to the Secretary of the Smithsonian Institution 1890–*

PLATE I
Photograph of Bat Creek Inscription

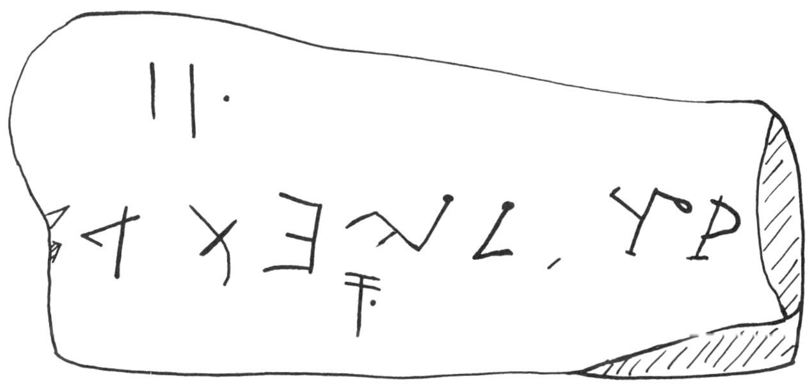

PLATE II
Facsimile of Bat Creek Inscription

'91, Government Printing Office, Washington, D.C., 1894, pp. 392–394 and figures 272, 273): "Nothing of interest was discovered until the bottom was reached, where nine skeletons were found lying on the original surface of the ground, surrounded by dark colored earth. These were disposed as shown in Fig. 272. No. 1 lying at full length with the head south, and close by,

parallel with it, but with the head north, was No. 2. On the same level were seven others, all lying close side by side, with heads north and in a line. All were badly decayed. No relics were found with any but No. 1, immediately under the skull and jaw bones of which were two copper bracelets,[5] an engraved stone, a small drilled fossil,[6] a copper bead, a bone implement,[7] and some small pieces of polished wood. The earth about the skeletons was wet and the pieces of wood soft and colored green by contact with the copper bracelets.[8] The bracelets had been rolled in something, probably bark, which crumbled away when they were taken out. The engraved stone lay partially under the back part of the skull and was struck by the steel prod used in probing."

It is important that all the objects were found undisturbed *in situ*, under the skull of the main personage: the only one headed south and at the same time the only one buried with objects. It looks as though the person next to him (his wife?) and the other seven (his children and/or key personnel?) were killed to accompany him in the afterlife. The text, as we shall note, may provide a possible clue to their motivation.

The Smithsonian has kept the group of finds together so that they can be studied. The wooden fragments, which seem to have formed part of a small disk-like object, have traces of copper oxide, suggesting that the wood was sheathed in copper (to serve quite probably as earplugs). The wood and the bone implement should yield Carbon-14 dates, and I have requested the Smithsonian to perform the tests as soon as possible. Another object in the group is a ferrous paint-stone (not mentioned by Thomas), which when rubbed yields a red powder, that if mixed with a suitable vehicle such as oil, could be used to color one's skin.

The most significant find is of course the inscribed stone which Thomas published upside down (on p. 394) and erroneously surmised to be in the Cherokee script. The Cherokee syllabary, which was devised by Sequoya in 1821, has nothing to do with the Bat Creek text.[9] What misled Thomas was the dogmatic, and false, thesis of the whole *Annual Report*, that the Mound Indians, as far back as their remains can be found archeologically, are the same as the present day Indians such as the Cherokees. All of the evidence runs counter to the notion of a static population throughout pre-Columbian America, and specifically in our Southeast.[10]

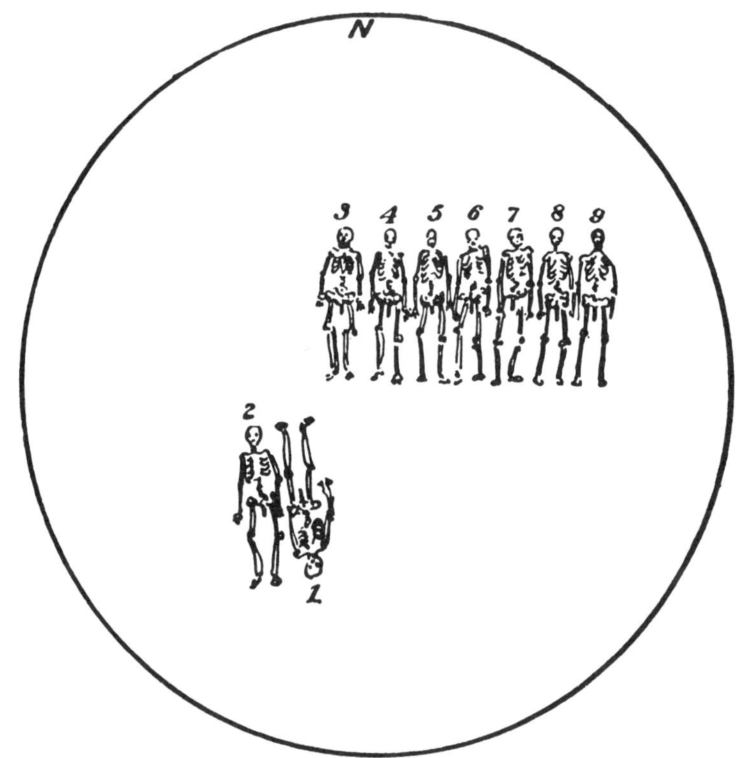

PLATE III
Disposition of Skeletons, Burial Mound, No. 3, Bat Creek,
Loudon County, Tennessee

In 1950 the late Dr. W. W. Strong recorded on worksheets that the Bat Creek text is in "Phoenician" script when viewed right-side up. Strong's unpublished discovery was used by his friend Joseph Corey Ayoob who read three letters (LYH) correctly in his *Ancient Inscriptions in the New World* (P.O.B. 626, Aliquippa, Pa., 1964).

The next person to observe that the Bat Creek text, if read right-side up, has "Phoenician" letters, is a patent lawyer, Henriette Mertz in her book *The Wine Dark Sea* (published by the author, Box 207, Old Post Office, Chicago 60690, 1964, p. 130). Like Chief Justice John Haywood, Dr. Mertz is trained to weigh evidence. Her work (like Ayoob's) went unnoticed, partly be-

LETTER FORMS

BAT CREEK	MODERN HEBREW	CLOSEST FORMS ON MESHORER'S JEWISH COINS (##5-36 = MACCABEAN, ##148-164 = FIRST REBELLION, #165-215 = SECOND REBELLION) OR OTHER SOURCES AS INDICATED

I. IDENTIFIED LETTERS

ᚎ	א	ᚎ (#148), ᚎ (##149, 169, 179, 180)
ᚃ	ד	ᚃ (##28, 152)
Ⅎ	ה	Ⅎ (##27, 154)
⅄	ו	⅄ (#154)
∿	י	∿ (#159), ∿ (#154)
∠	ל	∠ (##148, 200, 201)

II. PROBLEMATIC LETTERS

‖	נ	‖ (##18A, 22, 23)

	ז	⊨, ⊣ (Levy, *Jüdische Münzen*, p. 137)
₱		or
	ק	⊢ (#154)

	ק	⊢ (#148), ⊢ (#164), ⊢ (#151)
⅄°		or
	צ	Cf. Cursive Forms in the Qumran Manual of Discipline: ℥ (1:6), ℥ (4:2) & Habakkuk Commentary: ⅄ (1:14), ⅄ (4:11)

III. POSSIBLE RESTORATION OF BROKEN LETTER

ᚃ	מ	℈ (#30) & The Older Form ℈ (Levy, *op. cit.*, p. 136)

PLATE IV

cause her drawing of the text was inaccurate, and she identified only two of the Canaanite letters correctly. It remained for a professional Americanist, Dr. Joseph B. Mahan, Jr., to rediscover independently the Canaanite identity of the Bat Creek Inscription. In August 1970, Mahan wrote to me that on inverting the published text, he found that a sequence of five letters matched up with a Canaanite alphabet chart in the *Cambridge Ancient History*.

He was right about the first three letters: ליה . Instead of sending me a handdrawn facsimile, he enclosed with his letter an excellent picture of the text made by a Smithsonian photographer. This time there was no mistaking the nature of the inscription.

While there is no question concerning the identity of the ל , י and ה , they could appear in this form in several different periods. It is the next letter that fixes the chronology more precisely; this form of ו is found on coins of Roman date. This in turn showed that the fifth letter is not an imperfectly made א , but a ד , so that we can read the five letter sequence as ליהוד "for Judea." יהוד "Judea" is attested since the Achaemenian period (Daniel 2:25, 5:13 (*bis*); 6:14; Ezra 5:1, 8; 7:14). It occurs as יהד on all of the six known Hebrew coins of the fourth century B.C. (Meshorer, *op cit.*, pp. 116–117, plate I).

The Bat Creek text, however, has traces of a letter after ליהוד . The traces are not compatible with the forms of the ה and י of this inscription and accordingly preclude the obvious readings ליהוד ⸢ה⸣ or ליהוד ⸢י⸣ [ם] . However, the traces might possibly reflect מ so that ליהוד ⸢ם⸣ "For the Jews" is conceivable though not without difficulties (for יהודים or יהדים , with two yods, is how "Jews" is written on the Maccabean coins; note Meshorer, *op. cit.*, nos. 14, 18, 20, 21, 24, 25). Yet this difficulty is not insurmountable, for there is a tendency in the orthography of the biblical text to indicate consonantally only one of two long vowels that occur in the same word; thus *yᵉhûdîm* could conceivably appear as יהודם as well as יהדים. There are other problems that we should note though we cannot solve them now. Though the Second Commonwealth called itself "Jewish" (note יהוד in the Persian Period, and יהודים in the Persian and Maccabean Periods), the coins of the First (66–70 A.D.) and Second (132–135 A.D.) Rebellions against Rome consistently refer to the nation as "Israel." This anticipates (for whatever reason) the decision of the modern nation of Israel, which purposely avoided "Judah" (and its derivatives like "Jews" or "Jewish") to avoid confusion with the Jews of the Diaspora. The appearance of ליהוד⸢ים⸣ (instead of לישראל) on the Bat Creek Stone may therefore turn out to be significant.

A stylistic feature of the Bat Creek script also ties in with the use of the drill to embellish the letters (and symbols) on Hebrew coins of Roman times. Compare the drill marks on top of the י and ל with those on nos. 151, 154 and 155 (First Rebellion) and nos. 159, 163, 185, 188, 190, 190A, 204, 205, 207 etc. (Second Rebellion) in Meshorer's publication.

The first two letters, preceding the word-divider, are problematic. The one on the right could be a ק , except for the little horizontal stroke at the bottom (though a drilled dot there would not be unparalleled). The letter on the left could be צ in cursive Hebrew (such as we find in the Dead Sea Scrolls from Qumran). The reading ק צ . ליהוד [ ], would make sense if it were tenable paleographically. קץ "end" has had the technical meaning "the end of days (inaugurating the Golden or Messianic Age)" since at least the time when Daniel 12:4 was written;[11] there the "end" (קץ) marks the resurrection when "many of those asleep in the land of dust will wake up (*yāQîṢû*)." There is a conscious play on קץ "end" and the verb יקיץ "will wake." This interpretation would explain the character of the Bat Creek burial, with nine persons interred together apparently going to sleep in the earth expecting to wake for the resurrection. The א on the last line (see the "Letter Forms" chart) is followed by a dot apparently to show that it is not to be pronounced phonetically but read as the numeral "1." Now it happens that on the coins struck during the rebellions against Rome, such letters are used to designate the years of the new era. Thus Nos. 148–150 in Meshorer's *corpus*, have an א below the legend to indicate the first year (i.e., 66 A.D.) of the First Rebellion (66–70 A.D.). It is interesting to note that א so used, stands alone, while other year-letters are preceded by ש (for שנת); Nos. 151 and 152 have שב = שתם שנת (No. 153) "year 2." Nos. 154–155 have שג = שלש שנת (Nos. 156–157) "year 3." Nos. 158–160 have שד = ארבע שנת (Nos. 161–163) "year 4." No. 164 marks the closing days of the ill-starred War with שה "year 5." Bar Kokhba coins also indicate the year of the era (i.e., of the War). Thus the regular way of indicating the second year of the War (133 A.D.) is שב לחר standing for (ירושלים/) ישראל לחרות שתם שנת "year 2 of the Freedom of Israel (or Jerusalem)."

The paleographic objections to reading קץ are, as we have noted, twofold. First there is no other example of a ק with a horizontal stroke at the base; and second, we should not posit a *cursive* צ in a lapidary text.

My student Robert Stieglitz suggests another reading: זק . M. A. Levy (*op. cit.*, p. 137) records only one letter with a loop above, and a non-vertical line below; to wit, the ז which he records in two variant shapes as noted on our chart of "Letter Forms." (Unfortunately, all the examples of ז in the published facsimiles and photographs of the coins are not sufficiently legible.) ליהוד . זק "A Comet for Judea (/the Jew[s])" would make sense. For זק "comet," see *Aruch Completum* (by Nathan ben Yehi'el, ed. Alexander Kohut, Menorah, Vienna, 1926, vol. 3, p. 312). The Prophet Balaam (Numbers 24:17) predicted that a "Star" would arise from Jacob and annihilate Israel's foes: "I see him, though not now; I behold him, though he's not near. A Star (כוכב) proceeds from Jacob; e'en a Planet (שבט)[12] from Israel, who shall smite the corners of Moab, yea smash all the Sons of Seth." To Jews oppressed by Rome, Moab could only refer to Rome, and the Star referred to the Messianic figure destined to save God's People from Rome. This is how Simon came to be called Bar Kokhba "Son of the Star." By the same token,

זק "(The) Comet" would quite appropriately describe the

Savior who would usher in the Messianic Age in fulfillment of

Balaam's prophecy. By reading זק "Comet" the interpretation

of the text would remain essentially the same: "Year 1 of the Comet for Judea (/the Jew[s])": i.e., the dawn of the Golden Age. This would explain how the nine persons were buried simultaneously; they may have willingly perished together in the expectation of resurrection in the First Year of the Messianic salvation, to witness the Golden Age for the Jews as prophesied in Scripture.[13]

The importance of the Bat Creek inscription at this time is that the circumstances of its discovery obliges us to widen our concept of the geographic horizons of Roman influence which extended to the Western Hemisphere.[14] And the same holds true for the Jews who rebelled twice against the Roman Empire.

Before we can place these facts into the perspective of documented Old World history, we have to get over the stereotypes of "Jewish landlubbers" and "Romans with no real talent for seamanship." Such generalities are always misleading, and these particular ones have contributed to the inability of historians to reconstruct a realistic world history reckoning with the transoceanic migrations of antiquity. Ancient Israel had, according to Biblical evidence, no less than three tribes devoted to navigation: Zebulun (Genesis 49:13) and Dan and Asher (Judges 5:17). The proudest moment in Israel's secular achievements was the Solomonic Age when Israel and Tyre launched joint merchant marine expeditions to distant lands, some requiring three years for the round trip (1 Kings 10:22). Israelite partnership with the Phoenicians continued for many centuries, as spelled out in detail by Robert Stieglitz in his 1971 Brandeis Ph.D. dissertation *Maritime Activity in Ancient Israel* (available at University Microfilms Inc., Ann Arbor, Michigan). Here we need only bridge the gap between the tenth century B.C. (when Hiram's and Solomon's fleets embarked from Ezion-geber on bold oceanic ventures) and the Jewish rebellions against Rome.

In the fifth century B.C., Herodotus twice refers to the "Syrians of Palestine." In *Histories* 2:104, he describes them as practising circumcision. A Palestinian people singled out for the rite of circumcision can only be the Jews. Now in 7:89 Herodotus states that the main contingent of the Persian navy of 1207 triremes was the unit of 300 triremes supplied by Phoenicians and Syrians of Palestine showing that Jewish seamanship in concert with the Phoenicians was not a thing of the past.

During the Roman period, Jewish coins sometimes feature maritime objects such as ships and anchors. Thus Meshorer (*op. cit.*, p. 69) observes that "the most notable feature of the coins of Archelaus [4 B.C.–6 A.D.] is the special character of their designs. Of six types of different coins that he struck, five bear clear maritime symbols (nos. 56, 57, 58, 59, 60), due perhaps to his having inherited from his father the two principal harbour cities of Caesarea and Jaffa." The portrayal of ships on those coins reflects the naval interests of the Jews, and their need for harbors such as those at Caesarea and Jaffa.

During the First Rebellion, the Romans scored a naval victory over a large Jewish fleet at Jaffa; 4200 bodies of drowned Jews were counted according to Josephus' description of the battle (*Jewish War* 3:419 ff.). That Josephus is not blowing up a minor engagement into a major catastrophe is proved by the fact that not only the victorious Caesar, Vespasian, but also his two sons and successors, Titus and Domitian, struck coins to celebrate their great *Victoria Navalis* over *Judaea Navalis* (the Latin legends appear individually on their coins).[15] The ships depicted on the walls of Masada and of Beit Shearim are not to be explained away as casual designs or religious symbols; they reflect the real naval concerns and activities of the Jews.

The reconstruction of history can only be obstructed by entrenched blind spots. No useful purpose is served in perpetuating stereotypes such as "Athenians were philosophers and artists," "Spartans were bloodthirsty and unspiritual," "Philistines were philistine," "Hebrews were Prophets and farmers," "Phoenicians were all sailors," etc. The Phoenicians included such good farmers that Mago's great work on agriculture was ordered translated from Punic into Latin by the Roman Senate. The tribe of Dan is chided in the Song of Deborah (Judges 5:17) for "dwelling in ships" instead of joining the land-minded tribes in their struggle against Jabin and Sisera. The plain fact is that significant segments of Jewry continued to engage in navigation throughout antiquity, the Middle Ages and into the Age of Discovery. Henry the Navigator drew heavily on Jewish naval talent including the important school of naval instrumentation and cartography fostered by the Jews of Majorca. Nor was Jewish seamanship limited to such lofty scientific levels; there were also Jewish pirates at large in the Mediterranean.

How are we to explain the distorted picture that we find in the standard histories? Jewish involvement in maritime affairs had declined to the vanishing point by the nineteenth century when the foundations of modern historiography were laid, and the stereotype of the nineteenth cenutry Jew was to a great extent retrojected into the past. The same may have happened, *mutatis mutandis*, with the Romans. By the nineteenth century the great maritime Italian cities had long fallen into decline, and Italy had not yet recaptured any of its ancient Roman glory. It is only in this twentieth century that modern Italy can boast of naval prowess. Moreover, we exaggerate the dichotomy between the Roman land power and the Punic sea power. As school children many of us got the impression that Rome was inept on the sea, *vis-à-vis* the Carthaginians and Etruscans who were mariners. But Roman tradition, as enshrined in the Aeneid, has the Romans coming to Italy by sea. More prosaic is the hard fact that the Romans were obliged to learn the arts of seamanship from their nautical rivals and enemies; and they learned their lessons well. Only a naval power could rule the Mediterranean and call that Sea *Mare Nostrum*. Nor is it too much to expect of historians that they reckon with the undeniable fact that Palestine is a coastal country whose historic importance is predicated on two geographical facts related to trade. Not only is it the only landbridge between the world's two largest continents; but it also has ports on the Mediterranean that lead to the Atlantic and on the Red Sea that lead to the Indian Ocean and beyond. Until the nautical dimension is adequately understood, there can be no real history of Israel, nor a real history of Rome, nor any real history of antiquity.

FOOTNOTES

1. This article does not imply that the contacts discussed are the first or the last between the Eastern and Western Hemispheres. To put the subject in its broad historic context, see my *Before Columbus: Links between the Old World and Ancient America*, Crown Publishers, New York, 1971.
2. I.e., Antoninus Pius (138–161 A.D.) and Marcus Aurelius (161–180 A.D.).
3. Reigned 180–192 A.D.
4. Unlike the Roman coins seen and described by Haywood, the Bar Kokhba coins are still available for examination; the names and addresses of the finders who still have them have been published in the *Courier-Journal* articles. Mr. Samuel Dyen has kindly called to my attention a recapitulation that appeared on 17 April 1967 in the New York Yiddish newspaper *The Day-Jewish Journal*.
5. [The bracelets are in fact brass (an alloy of copper and zinc) rather than copper. Brass was used by the Romans, in addition to bronze (an alloy of copper and tin).—C.H.G.]
6. [The crinoid fossil has the shape of a small cylinder.—C.H.G.]
7. [The implement comes to a point and could have been used as a spear point or awl.—C.H.G.]
8. [The green coloration probably came from copper sheathing on the wooden object, rather than from the brass bracelets.—C.H.G.]
9. The Cherokee syllabary is reproduced by David Diringer, *The Alphabet*, 3rd ed., Funk & Wagnalls, New York, 1968, vol. 2, p. 132.
10. Part of the problem is the foundationless but often tacitly assumed notion that the Indians are of one race. A more realistic definition of "American Indians" is "all the inhabitants of the Western Hemisphere in 1492 (and their descendants)." The ethnic components of the pre-Columbian Americans are numerous and the racial mixtures virtually infinite.
11. It has this meaning in the *Manual of Discipline* 4:25, in the Thirteen Principles of Maimonides (מחכי קץ ישועתו "those who hope

for His End-of-Salvation"), and in the traditional Hanukka hymn known by its opening words מעוז צור (to wit, קץ בבל זרבבל לקץ שבעים נושעתי "the end of Babylon; Zerubbabel! At the end of the seventy (years of captivity) I was saved.").

12. Since שבט is here parallel to "star," it must have been intended to convey the sense familiar to us from postbiblical שביט "planet."

13. The two vertical lines followed by a dot, at the top of the inscription, are enigmatic. They might stand for the numeral "2," but then we would have to explain what the numeral referred to, since the year "1" is indicated. Another possibility is take each vertical line as the letter נ , which is sometimes written on the coins; e.g., both נ's in יהוחנן on No. 18A of Meshorer, *op. cit.*, pl. III. נ (whose numerical value is "50") is a sacred letter according to *Manual of Discipline* 10:4. Since the meaning of נ *"nûn"* is "fish," Joan K. Gordon makes the interesting suggestion that the double נ נ may be zodiacal "Pisces" regularly portrayed as two fish.

14. The evidence for this is manysided and includes the testimony of classical authors (cf. *Before Columbus*); nor is there any valid counter-indication. It is the clear-cut archeological context of an inscription in a Mediterranean script of Roman date, found in America, that gives the Bat Creek Stone its special significance.

15. This is documented by Stieglitz, *op. cit.*, "Introduction."

The teaching of Hippocrates that disease in general may arise either from the food we eat or the air we breathe generally prevailed all through the Middle Ages and even later. Therefore when a disease seized a large number of different persons of varied ages and sexes at one time, it was considered that it must have taken its origin from the air. This theory was approved by Galen who added that climatic factors also contribute to the outbreak of the malady. Miasmata, given off by water in certain communities, "taint the air and occasion disease."

Benjamin Lee Gordon, M.D.: Medieval and Renaissance Medicine, New York, 1959, p. 457.

CHAPTER 2

*Allergy and Ecology**

by

GORDON P. BAKER, M.D.**

Allergy is deeply concerned with ecology and is in effect the study of ecological disease. I feel it will be helpful to your understanding of environment, pollution and health to gain insights from the allergist's point of view although I shall not confine my presentation strictly to allergy.

Allergy may be defined as an altered or changed reaction of the body to a foreign substance that is ordinarily harmless. The immune system protects against invaders such as bacteria and viruses. Part and parcel of every bacterial or viral infection is the body's immune response and specific diseases are characterized by the nature and specificity of this response. Cancer and allergy in effect represent opposite ends of disease of the immune system. In cancer, the immune system is paralyzed and does not respond. In allergy, the immune system over-reacts to ordinarily harmless substances such as pollen and foods. The immune response, then, is "turned on" by the allergic reaction with resulting disease whereas it is "turned off" by cancer.

What are the allergic diseases? How common are they? What

---

*Presented before an Ecology Seminar at the University of Washington in Seattle on May 28, 1971.

**Gordon P. Baker, M.D. is an Allergist practicing in Seattle, Washington. He is a member of the faculty of the Medical School of the University of Washington.

causes them? What relevance do they have with our concern with ecology, pollution and health? Probably half (50%) of the population have an allergic problem. One quarter (25%) have a problem severe enough to require treatment. Fourteen percent (14%) have hay fever, 2% have asthma and less than 1% have eczema.

The part of the body affected by allergy is called the shock organ. In hay fever the shock organ is the nose; in chronic sinusitis it is the sinuses; in asthma it is the lungs.

In gastrointestinal allergy the result may be colic in infancy, chronic stomach pain, nausea, even ulcers, colitis, chronic diarrhea or constipation. I might mention that gastrointestinal allergy is a frequently misdiagnosed entity.

Any part of the body may be affected by allergy. The eyes may become itchy, runny or swollen. Allergy of the ear causing serous otitis media is a leading cause of deafness in children. Allergy of the skin may manifest itself by eczema, urticaria or hives as with poison ivy. Allergy of the bladder may manifest itself by bedwetting which is sometimes erroneously blamed on emotional problems. Allergy of the central nervous system may take many forms, the most common of which is tension fatigue. Emotional reactions are frequently present as an effect of allergy rather than as a cause.

Chronic rhinosinusitis, chronic bronchitis and asthma are highly affected by air pollution.

The causes of allergy include inhalants like pollens, ingestants like foods and drugs and infections. It is worthy of note that nature has supplied us with natural "air pollution." We live in a sea of germs and pollens from trees, grass or weeds. Looking at it this way, hay fever may be defined as the end result when a person's nose gets in the way of the sexual life of plants. Airborne mold spores can cause serious disease. Knowledge of the specific pollens for a given area is essential. Animal dander from cats and dogs affect some people.

Mankind has had millions of years to adapt to these outside natural pollutents but has had only two decades or less to attempt to adapt to the new synthetics and chemicals released in the air. An analogy might here be made with the unfortunate situation of the Eskimo who has lived in isolation in a bacteriologically protected environment for many centuries and to whom ordinary measles introduced into his village from the outside may produce as high as a fifty percent (50%) mortality. Our ancestors unquestionably had similar experiences but those who survived were capable of resisting measles.

I feel that pollution in the home is every bit as important as outside pollution. Housedust is a major allergen throughout the civilized world. Recently it has been found that an insect, the housedust mite, is the major allergen of housedust. Many homes in the Puget Sound area have forced hot air heat which is fired by gas or oil and which is disseminated throughout the house via air ducts. From an allergic standpoint this is the worst possible kind of heat for it circulates and re-circulates all the dust, mold, animal dander and products of combustion throughout the house. It is impossible to keep a home clean from an allergic standpoint with forced hot air heat. Many thousands of people in the Puget Sound area are ill, some of them quite severely so, because of this type of heating system. You would have to visit an allergist's office to imagine the magnitude of this problem. I feel that hot air heat as now provided should be declared illegal and I wonder if the manufacturers and contractors involved might be liable under products liability law for making people sick. It is possible to clean some hot air systems with an electrostatic dust precipitator, but most systems in my patients' homes are improperly constructed with an inadequate return ducting, so an air cleaner is not mechanically feasible.

Many mattresses are stuffed with cotton felting and their manufacture can cause a severe form of chronic inflammatory and fibrotic lung disease known as byssinosis which is an occupational hazard among workers in the textile industry.

Tobacco smoke is a subject in itself. Each cigarette represents 14.5 minutes off of one's life. Tobacco kills about 60,000 a year with lung cancer which is more then the Viet Nam War has killed to date. Many thousands die each year from emphysema. The heart attack rate is 3 or 4 times higher in people who smoke. Cancer of the bladder is related to tobacco smoke. If the mother smokes during pregnancy there is a higher incidence of premature babies with respiratory distress.

Not only does tobacco bother the addict, or habituate, but also people around him. It has been shown that children have more respiratory infections when the parents smoke and the frequency of such infections is directly proportional to the quantity of smoke inhaled. Many people are allergic to tobacco smoke and become very ill when they are in a room with smokers. I have seen a significant number of people who have had to give up their jobs because of this problem. I feel that there should be specific laws regarding smoking in public places and places of employment. The allergic person's civil rights have long been overlooked.

The lungs and sinuses are lined by motile ciliated epithelial cells and are covered with a blanket of mucous created by mucous cells. This results in a constantly moving fine blanket of mucous which cleanses and protects the lungs. Ciliated cells grown in tissue culture resemble a field of wheat rippling in the wind. When tobacco smoke is placed over the normally motile cilia, they become paralyzed and stop all movement.

I desire here to interject several concepts of importance to our topic: one is the cumulative total effect in which several damaging substances combine together to cause more damage then any one of the components. Smoking aggravates air pollution, industrial disease and allergic disease. A person who smokes 3 packs of cigarettes a day, lives in Los Angeles, has asthma and works with asbestos has certainly had it. Chronic recurrent respiratory infections aggravate illness and cause direct damage to sinus or lung tissue. The incidence of respiratory infections is much higher where individuals have untreated allergy and are exposed to air pollutents.

There are many different methods by which substances may produce disease: In the allergic reaction there is a definite antigen-antibody reaction. There may be a toxic effect as when arsenic, mercury or lead directly poison cells. There may be an irritant effect as with one of my pediatric patients who inhaled a large amount of pepper into his lungs and was practically moribund when I saw him. Some of the gases in pollution unquestionably have damaging or irritating effects. Other substances may have pharmacologic or drug effects. There may be an overdose effect as when a drug or substance may be harmless in one quantity but dangerous in a larger quantity.

Asthma is difficulty in breathing manifested by wheezing respirations. In such patients the bronchi are in spasm, there is tissue swelling or edema and the mucous in the chest is thickened. These three things combine to produce lung obstruction which makes the asthmatic a high risk patient when his already compromised lungs are exposed to air pollution.

Asthma is usually reversible. That is, with treatment, lung function tests will improve.

Chronic obstructive lung disease or emphysema is manifested by irreversibly decreased pulmonary function. Chronic obstructive lung disease is usually not allergic, but occasionally may be the end result of long standing allergic problems.

The two fastest growing causes of death in the United States are chronic bronchitis and chronic obstructive lung disease caused by tobacco smoke and industrial pollution.

As far as food allergy is concerned, there are over 2300 additives in food. I have traced allergy to only a few additives such as monosodium glutamate, cyclamates and food colors. I should emphasize that for the relatively few patients I have seen with cyclamate intolerance I have seen many allergic to other common foods such as milk or bread. If the FDA applied the same logic explained in removing cyclamates from the marketplace to standard food substances, they could well remove milk, bread, eggs, corn, chocolate and orange juice from the marketplace. There are many proven diseases directly caused by allergy and pollution but we should avoid hysteria over unproven substances. Much more study of the various food additives is indicated.

Environmental lung disease should be preventable. Among the common occupationally caused pulmonary diseases are: (1) silicosis, a form of pneumoconiosis (a fibrous induration of the lungs due to the irritation caused by the inhalation of dust incident to various occupations) due to the inhalation of stone dust as in stone masons' disease and potters' consumption, (2) anthracosis, a form of pneumoconiosis due to the inhalation of coal dust or coal miners' disease and (3) asbestosis, a form of pneumoconiosis occurring among workers in asbestos factories. Asbestos can also cause lung cancer and benign and malignant mesotheliomata (growths derived from the living cells of the pleura). Smoking increases the incidence of lung cancer among asbestosis victims 90 fold. It is significant that asbestos bodies are found in the lungs of people not exposed occupationally. This suggests a relationship to air pollution.

Beryllium, an elemental white metal belonging to the alkaline earths, can cause granulomas and malignancies in the lungs of animals. Among humans, there have been reactions to as little as 1% Beryllium in some copper alloys. Cadmium oxide may cause an acute pneumonitis with a high mortality rate.

Irritant gases containing ammonia, nitrogen oxide, zinc chloride, chlorine and phosphine are all known to cause serious acute problems but their long term effects have not been adequately evaluated.

I have been extremely interested in one pollutant, TDI or toluene di-isocyanate. This is used to make polyurethane foam and surely causes lung disease and allegedly heart disease.

Outdoor dust does not seem to cause great problems. Moldy hay may cause a disease called Farmer's Lung which is a true allergic reaction to a specific species of mold spores. Pigeon breeder's disease is a similar process and is caused by an allergy to substances in pigeon droppings and serum.

Textile dusts are of vital importance. Cotton, flax or hemp will cause byssinosis which gives rise to such symptoms as tightness of the chest and coughing and wheezing on the first work day after an absence from work. Constant exposure may result in chronic obstructive lung disease. Twenty-nine percent (29%) of the workers in southern textile mills are affected by byssinosis. This gives rise to the estimation that about 17,000 textile workers in the south presently are affected by this disease.

There are various inert dusts such as fiberglass, glass wool and rayon. These substances, while giving rise to acute problems, are hard to evaluate for long term effects.

Enzyme detergents should be banned from the marketplace. It was substantiated at least two years ago that workers in factories producing the enzymes which are a bacterial product, were having episodes of asthma and obstructive lung disease. At a recent meeting of the American Academy of Allergy an entire afternoon symposium was devoted to these enzymes and it was recommended that they be banned at once. It is an interesting commentary that *Consumer Reports* indicates that such enzymes are ineffective in helping with cleansing.

I have recently seen a patient rendered allergic to cork dust employed in packing missiles. Wood and paper products may cause lung disease of varying severity. One of my most severely ill patients with chronic obstructive lung disease has a long history of exposure to flour dust. He recently developed severe respiratory failure after he cut and prepared 45 bushels of onions to be used in a frozen food product. Baker's asthma is a major problem in the grain industry. Book bindery dust may cause much trouble as will library dust or dust from old books. Not too many of my patients die, but two sawmill operators, each having 30 years or more exposure to sawdust, have been fatalities. Construction dust, sawdust, cardboard dust and newsprint may all bother various people and cause varying degrees of sickness.

A tragic case was that of a girl who started working in a beauty shop at age 18 and arrived at the hospital dead on admission from chronic lung disease and terminal respiratory failure at age 26. Beautician's lung disease caused by chronic exposure to hair spray is a major problem. Many other cosmetics cause trouble. I have seen several men with sinusitis caused directly by their wives' hair sprays.

Among machinists, cutting oil may cause trouble. A ship's engineer aboard a Washington State ferry has severe respiratory problems because of the poor ventilation in the ship's engine room. The engine room apparently sucks in air directly from the car decks, an example of poor design. Other occupational lung problems may occur in iron workers, welders and chemists.

Patients customarily fill out a questionaire before I see them and it is surprising that so many know what they are allergic to even prior to the first examination. According to their own estimation out of 200 patients selected at random from my files, 36.5% stated that they were rendered allergically ill by house dust, 25% by respiratory infections, 19% by grass, 13.5% by tobacco smoke, 12.5% by perfume, 12% by animal hair, 11% by hair spray, 9.5% by sawdust, 8.5% by smog, 7.5% by fumes, 6.9% by books, 6% by automobile exhaust, 4.5% by grain dust and Christmas trees, 4% by wood smoke and 2.5% by newspapers. These percentages would be low as compared to those ascertained after diagnostic studies are completed.

I have not had any direct experience with water pollution. Patients living in the vicinity of the airport complain about noise pollution and the opinion has been expressed by competent authorities that noise pollution is an important form of pollution.

As far as treatment is concerned a prime principle of both treatment of allergy and industrial disease is prevention. All industrial diseases are theoretically preventable. Proper filtration equipment is currently available to eliminate allergens. Elimination of offending items such as cats or dogs from the house can be carried out effectively. Allergy desensitization injections are given for such things as pollens. Aside from its prevention, there is no specific medical treatment for air pollution other than leaving the offending area or providing air cleaners in the home.

Presently it would appear that tobacco smoke is the main cause of chronic lung disease including both chronic bronchitis and emphysema. Many of the chemicals found in tobacco smoke are also found in air pollution. With increasing air pollution we are actually seeing more and more chronic lung disease.

Time is running short and immediate action is vital.

My mother, Mrs. Dorothy Gordon, was the greatest inspiration of my life. She died in 1955 at the age of 75. My father, Dr. Benjamin Lee Gordon, was not only a noted medical historian, author and ophthalmologist, but a father who was a rock of strength at all times. He died in 1965 at the age of 94.

My mother's message to her progeny emphasized the importance of integrity, humanity and philanthropy as prime factors in our daily lives. My father's clearly indicated that scholarship and erudition must be combined with tradition and service to mankind to assure a good and constructive life. Both were in complete agreement that worldly goods were of very minor import in achieving happiness and fulfillment. It is noteworthy that my parents' philosophy has deeply permeated the characters of all of their children and grandchildren and, I note with joy, has reached down even unto the souls of their great grandchildren.

Dr. Benjamin Lee Gordon's bibliography included three standard volumes on the history of medicine: (1) "The Romance of Medicine," (2) "Medicine Throughout Antiquity" and (3) "Medieval and Renaissance Medicine," a biography, "Between Two Worlds: The Memoirs of a Physician," and numerous articles on clinical ophthalmology and the history of medicine published in the *Archives of Ophthalmology* and various other medical journals. He was a contributor to the Encyclopedia Britannica and Collier's Encyclopedia.

The What and Why of the Gordon Medical Scholarship Program by Maurice B. Gordon, M.D. *Medical Times*, Vol. 98, No. 10, Oct. 1970, pp. 99–100.

It is difficult to draw sharply defined lines in demarcating the beginning and ending of the Medieval Period. Old textbooks usually refer to the year 476 A.D. (the date of the final fall of Rome) as the start of this epoch and the year 1453 A.D. (the date of the fall of Constantinople) as the termination. This antiquated designation of a period of a thousand years is purely arbitrary.

The deposition of Romulus Augustulus, the last Roman Emperor in the West, in the year 476, was certainly not one of those events upon which the cultural history of the Western World depended. It did not even mark the final end of the Roman Empire for imperial unity was restored two years later for a short period. Likewise European culture did not suddenly regain ascendancy with the fall of Constantinople for the new conquerors of the Eastern Empire, the Turks, had little ambition for cultural advancement. To the contrary, their conquest of the Arabic countries extinguished the last vestige of Saracen civilization. The trend of historical investigations leads one to doubt the validity of any medieval period where the evolution of man became altogether stagnant. The advance of society has always continued. Of course, progress has not always been uniform. There was retrogression when barbarous races superimposed their substandard civilizations.

The period between modern and ancient times, however, does include a period of roughly a millennium. During most of these years, civilization was dragged down to a low level and mankind, hopelessly restricted by the authority of the Church, frittered away its existence with war and monastic dreams.

From the fifth to the eleventh century little progress was made in Europe. This epoch, often referred to as the Dark Ages, was a period in history when the higher ideals of European learning were relegated to a very base position. Only faint glimmerings of the great European civilization that had died continued to flicker in the dark cells of the monasteries where worm-eaten volumes of the works of the ancient Greeks were preserved but seldom referred to.

The power of the old civilization to absorb the new races had been exhausted by the fifth century and consequently the political history of Europe turned toward a different path. The fifth century witnessed the actual dismemberment of the Roman Empire. The peoples of Spain, Gaul, parts of Italy and Britain began forming the rude beginnings of what were to become the European national states of later centuries. This revolution was of sufficient magnitude to be regarded as the opening of a dark new era.

Both secular and independent learning deteriorated but the greatest stagnation took place in the fields of philosophy and medicine. A certain type of religious philosophy (known as Scholasticism) absorbed the attention of many thinkers from about the eleventh to the fifteenth centuries. Historians often refer to Scholasticism as the only intellectual interest of the Middle Ages. Most medieval intellectuals concerned themselves with petty and undeterminable problems as, for instance, how many angels can stand at one time on the point of a needle. There were few medieval investigators who had true scientific eagerness—men like Roger Bacon, Duns Scotus and Occam were hopelessly outnumbered by those who were unscientific and uncritical in their learning.

Benjamin Lee Gordon, M.D.: Medieval and Renaissance Medicine, New York, 1959, pp. 1–2.

CHAPTER 3

What's New with Edmund Burke?

by

JONATHAN B. BAKER, A.B., LL.B.*

Edmund Burke (1729–1797), the great British conservative statesman and philosopher, insists that social systems function like very delicate machines and warns that to tamper with a single part of a social system for any purpose, however laudable, may produce unforeseen malfunctions in other parts.

Burke emphasizes that the most lasting effects of high moral causes may not even be detectable at their inception and that the eventual effects of more basely contrived programs may be excellent indeed. In the latter case, it is even possible for the deleterious early effects to be directly responsible for the eventual excellence.

Conversely, according to Burke, well-intentioned and benign programs which seem perfect at their commencement, may develop downright malignant and destructive conclusions. Burke also notes that obscure and almost latent causes can eventually give rise to a state's basic prosperity or depression.

Thus Burke notes the folly of attempting to destroy *in toto* any institution which has served to any tolerable degree for the common purposes of society over the ages or for synthetically entirely rebuilding such an institution without models and patterns of approved utility.[1]

---

*Jonathan B. Baker is a social planner in The Department of Social Planning and Community Development in Vancouver, B.C., Canada.

Liberal political and social thinkers, on the other hand, have proceeded from the optimistic if erroneous assumption that well-meaning technological or social interventions more likely than not improve the social system and that coincident deleterious effects will somehow take care of themselves.

The last fifty years is replete with examples of social and technological innovations that have produced unexpected and undesirable results because of the failure or inability of the innovators to take a comprehensive view of the systems being affected.

The automobile, for example, at the turn of the century was hailed as a device that would forever rid our cities of pollution, bring about a return of the populace to the farms and eliminate the unbearable congestion caused by horsedrawn carriages. Futurists of the era failed to recognize the fact that when a desirable thing is made available to everyone, its social utility is diminished for all.

Consider urban renewal: well meaning attempts to clear slums and replace them with more habitable housing projects resulted in violence in many cities because planners did not take into account the social disruptions caused by such renewal programs. And in the 1960s massive highway and transportation investments expanded the scale of problem solving and generated new social problems of even greater enormity.

Because so much social disruption has resulted from promising social innovations, not only is liberalism under attack, but more importantly, the very "idea of progress" itself is besieged. The notion that "things are generally getting better" did not form a part of classical Greek thinking nor was it part of the intellectual evaluation of other civilizations of antiquity and the Middle Ages. The Renaissance seems to have inspired the notion that change *per se* is beneficial.

Within the last few years however, concern for the environment has cast doubt on the value of technological progress, just as concern over the unforeseen effects of social change has cast doubt on the value of social change. When the deep rooted belief in the "idea of progress" is suddenly taken away, the effect of this change cannot be overestimated. From that moment we have no compass to guide us nor can we know to what port we steer.

SIMULATION STUDIES

The most modern concepts of urban planning which seek to utilize computer technology proceed from a conservative Burkian view of civilization, i.e., that the state is like an enormously complicated machine and that planning must take into account a great number of dependent and independent variables.

In "Systems Studies of Urban Regions," Goldberg and Holling state:

> "Complex systems are characterized not exclusively by their parts but by the interactions among these parts. It is because of the complexity of the interaction that it is so dangerous, if easier, to take a fragmental view, to look at an isolated piece of the system. By concentrating on one fragment and trying to optimize the performance of that fragment we find the rest of the system responds in unsuspected ways. A freeway is constructed as an efficient artery to move people and the unsuspected social interactions stimulate urban sprawl and inner city decay. A ghetto is replaced by low-income housing to revitalize the urban core, and disrupted social interactions trigger violence. A tax subsidy is given to attract industry and the environmental interactions deteriorate the quality of life through pollution. Increasingly, such narrow interventions demonstrate that the whole is not a simple sum of the parts."[2]

Current planning involving simulation studies seeks to identify all conceivable variables in the urban complex and then test the effects of changes or interventions on the total system. Thus, the computer people are great complexifiers and are doing precisely what Burke said ought to be done.

What is likely to be the effect of such a systems approach to urban planning? Will it result in even greater rates of social change?

I doubt it. It is more likely that multivariate analysis will result in more conservative social interventions for the very reasons given by Burke.

What the computer will do for social planners is to make them aware of the incredible complexity of the system and point out *possible* disruptions in seemingly unrelated parts. However, since so many of the variables in the social sector are not quantifiable, the systems approach does not assure accuracy.

Approaching a problem knowing a little about the whole system rather than a lot about a small portion of it, may warn planners that they are steering a course between Scylla and Charybdis, but this certainly does not give them accurate charts to assure a safe and successful voyage.

Computer technology will force planners to be cautious and will heighten their awareness of the possible consequences of action or inaction by government. It will also enhance awareness of the possible effects on the ecology and social systems of technological innovations so that when a new technological device threatens certain deleterious social effects on some parts of the system, governments may intervene to delay or prohibit such innovations.

Alvin Toffler in his recent book, "Future Shock,"[3] describes the thundering rate of change in which we are careening into the 21st century and prescribes a philosophy for man who must live in turmoil and thrive on change.

I believe that it is more likely that the impact of new techniques of planning, including simulation models, will be to bring about a rebirth of conservatism and reluctance to experiment with new interventions to solve human problems. In fact there is a possibility that planners will be so fearful of the dangers of unchartered shoals that they will not leave port.

FOOTNOTES

1. Edmund Burke: Reflections on the Revolution in France, N. Y., 1955.
2. Goldberg and Holling: Systems Studies of Urban Regions, unpublished paper, University of British Columbia, Vancouver, 1970.
3. Alvin Toffler: Future Shock, New York, 1970.

In the third and fourth centuries, Talmudic rabbis applied the term, "Mazikin" (harmers and demons) to those invisible beings that are in the air. "They (the mazikin)," said Abayye, "surround us on all sides as the earth does the root of the vine." Rabbi Levi, quoting Rabbi Yudin, stated: "Every inch of space in the air is filled with them; they are ready to strike persons and inflict disease". . ."The Lord has created angels to counteract the harmful effect of the mazikin." Abba Benjamin said: "If a man could see them, he would lack the strength to face them."

In the light of modern bacteriology, the aforementioned statements are significant. They sound more like far advanced observation than legendary utterances. The mere fact that, at a time when medicine was in its infancy, invisible demons were thought to be the etiological factor of disease was an important contribution to medical knowledge.

Of special significance is the second half of Rabbi Yudin's statement: "The Lord has created angels to counteract the harmful effect of the demon." To use again a bacteriologic figure, this recalls a kind of benevolent microbe ('phage) or phagocyte which destroys the malevolent bacteria. Thus one has a picture of pathogenic organisms and antibodies in the guise of demons and angels.

It is not intended to convey the idea that certain persons anticipated the germ theory as early as the beginning of the present era. The discovery of bacteriology is acknowledged to be the crowning glory of the nineteenth century. Still less is it desired to convey the impression that ancient physicians were aware of the theory of phagocytosis, which was advanced by Metchnikoff in 1882. It is desired only to point out that long before the microscope was invented, there were those who believed that disease was produced by invisible beings of a physical nature.

*　　*　　*　　*　　*　　*

The belief that biologic factors produced pathologic conditions in the body, does not mean that disease processes were completely divorced from superstition. The ancient world was credulous and, in order to impress the sick, some form of superstition was attached to the worm. It was believed that these extraneous invaders of the human body were agencies of the gods sent from the netherworld to punish those who attempted to thwart the divine will.

In Babylonia the administration of worm remedies was also associated with superstition. The Babylonian physician was careful to administer them at the appearance of the new moon. The writer has observed the practice of administering "worm seed" to children regularly on the first day of the lunar month, still prevalent in the small towns of Lithuania.

Benjamin Lee Gordon, M.D.: The Evolution of Biologic Pathology from Ancient Animistic Beliefs, *American Journal of Clinical Pathology*, Vol. 10, No. 11, November 1940, pp. 777–778.

Disease-producing spirits frequently disguised themselves as worms, insects, and other objects. The people of ancient Mesopotamia believed that toothache is caused by a worm. An incantation to rid the patient of the worm has long been known in its Babylonian version. In the recent French excavations at Mari, in the Middle Euphrates, the Hurrian version of such an incantation has been unearthed. Francois Thureau-Dangin, the distinguished French cuneiformist, has recently published the latter.

The aborigines of Guiana believe that the *Kenaimas*, as the evil spirits are called, disguise themselves as worms, insects, or even inanimate objects, and enter the bodies of men to cause them headache, toothache, and other bodily pains. "A spirit is eating my tooth," is the expression used for toothache. There is an old belief among savages that worms or insects are the cause of disease and death. This conception originated in the savage mind from the frequent occurrence of worms passing through the rectum during life, or maggots crawling on traumatized tissues or dead bodies. Traces of this belief may be seen in Job, which refers to the worms, "after my skin worms destroy this body." Indians of California had a notion that in case of disease, snakes and reptiles entered their bodies and gnawed their vitals.

Benjamin Lee Gordon, M.D.: The Romance of Medicine, Phila., 1944, pp. 8–9.

CHAPTER 4

Functional Immunity to Nematode Disease: A Review*

by

BENJAMIN LEE GORDON, II, A.B., M.A., Ph.D., M.D.**

Although infections due to parasitic nematodes are thought by many to be primarily problems in tropical medicine, they are not uncommon in temperate climates as well, and represent a class of infectious diseases of world-wide importance.

Since they are of great significance to world public health, and since by virtue of their size, complexity, and nearly impermeable cuticle, nematodes offer certain novel challenges to the host's immune responses, the nature of functional immunity to infections caused by these agents is a subject of high intrinsic interest to the immunologist. While it is easy to accept the notion that almost any antibody which will combine with the protein coat of a virus and mask its receptor sites will inactivate it, or that any antibody which will opsonize the polysaccharide capsule of a *pneumococcus* will subsequently allow phagocytic cells to ingest and destroy the bacterium, it is difficult to accept the notion that nearly any antibody directed against a component of a worm like *Ascaris lum-*

*Reprinted from *Annals of Allergy*, Vol. 25, March 1967. pp. 137–144.
**Dr. Benjamin Lee Gordon, II is author of Dyscrasias of Immunoglobulin Production: Their Impact on Modern Immunology and senior author of Essentials of Immunology.

bricoides would result in the destruction of this parasite by the host. Indeed, both experimental evidence and common sense suggest that only certain very special types of antibodies might exert deleterious effects on a parasite of this size and complexity. Other defense mechanisms, such as phagocytosis, are also rendered inoperable, or nearly so, in dealing with such a large and mobile invader.

Before proceeding further, the author wishes to define functional immunity as any immunologic response that confers protection from reinfection by the parasite or serves to eliminate the primary infection.

HISTORICAL HIGHLIGHTS

William Taliaferro and Asa Chandler were first to consider seriously the nature of immunity to helminthiasis. It was Chandler who recognized that stages in the growth of metazoa are frequently accompanied by changes in their antigenic make-up, and thus that new criteria were necessary for the analysis of host immunity to helminths. In considering these problems, he established many of the concepts that have been used subsequently to study host immunity to helminths. As early as 1932, he proposed that functional immune reactions to helminths might be directed against biochemical targets in the worm, such as enzymes, which would subsequently impair metabolic processes necessary to the well-being of the parasite.[1] This concept was expanded by Taliaferro and Sarles in a series of papers published from 1938 to 1942. These workers noted in their studies of the immune responses of the rat to the trichiurid nematode *Nippostrongylus braziliensis* that worms taken from immune rats were coated with precipitates at their external orifices. Further, they noted that worms derived from non-immune rats developed similar precipitates when they were incubated in serum from immune animals. Closer inspection showed that the intestinal tracts of these worms were lined with similar precipitates. It was presumed that these precipitates were antibodies directed against the excretion and secretion products of the parasitic worms which might have deleterious effects by mechanical blockage of their orifices and interference with such living proceses as nutrient uptake, respiration, excretion, or release of gametes.[2-4] *

The pioneering investigations summarized above have laid the groundwork for many subsequent studies in immunity to nematode diseases.

NATURE OF FUNCTIONAL ANTIGENS

It is evident that the antigenic makeup of so large a parasite as a nematode must be indeed complex; to separate functional antigens from the milieu of structural and other materials possessing inherent antigenic activity clearly represents a formidable task. Because of these considerations, attempts to isolate functional antigens from whole ground-up worms have usually resulted in failure. Attention has been paid primarily to the isolation of functional antigens from the secretions and excretions of parasitic nematodes in recent years.[5] These antigens are associated with living parasites. Special attention has also been given to parasite enzymes as potential functional antigens. Several examples follow:

Thorson approached the problem of immunity to *Nippostrongylus braziliensis* in the rat by incubating living infective larvae in suitable liquid media so as to collect their excretion and secretion products. He found that media which contain such products would precipitate when mixed with serum derived from rats which had recovered from an experimenal infection. When worms were incubated in sera from such rats, they accumulated precipitates at the external orifices; however, when these sera were first absorbed with media containing the excretions and secretions of the worms (referred to hereafter as E.S. products), the precipitates at the orifices of the worms developed to a far lesser extent and much more slowly. The foregoing observations suggested that the infected rat did produce antibodies directed against the secretions

---

*Other workers have shown that such antibody precipitates have not been deleterious to nematodes grown in culture, and the effects of antibody precipitates on the orifices of nematodes is still a matter of some controversy. The reader is referred to Jackson's experiments concerning the effects of antibody precipitates on vital functions of a nematode in culture. (Jackson, G. J.: The Parasitic Nematode, *Neoaplectana glaseri*, in Axenic Culture. I. Effects of Antibodies and Anthelmintics, Exp Parasitology 11:241, 1961.)

and excretions of the parasite. When E.S. medium was tested for its ability to immunize normal rats it was found that it did confer a significant increase in ability to resist the challenge infection. Thorson also observed that while serum from a rat rendered immune by experimental infection could immunize a normal rat, it lost this ability if it were absorbed previously with E.S. medium.[5-9] Mills and Kent have investigated immunity to *Trichinella spiralis* in the rat and mouse by studying the E.S. antigens of this helminth. These antigens were studied by immunoelectrophoresis and immunodiffusion against sera obtained from animals immunized by experimental infection. The E.S. antigens were fractionated by column chromatography on DEAE-Sephadex, obtaining at least four immunologically active fractions. Antibodies directed against E.S. antigens were found to appear in the sera of infected animals after 30 days, and to reach a peak titer in 50 days, as determined by precipitin tests. Antibodies directed against E.S. antigens were shown to lower significantly the recovery of viable larvae from the muscles of challenged mice, thus implicating these antigens in functional immunity to trichinosis.[10]

Although studies of E.S. antigens have been given much emphasis, other approaches have also yielded valuable observations. Thorson dissected out oesophagi from the dog hookworm *Ancylostoma caninum* and prepared extracts of these which he tested for enzymatic activity and for immunogenicity. Protease activity was found which was abolished by serum from animals immunized by experimental infection. When oesophageal extracts were used to immunize dogs against challenge infections, the dogs so immunized were protected to some extent, as evidenced by reduced parasite burdens and marked stunting of the worms recovered.[11]

Evidence for antigenicity of the nematode cuticle has been presented by Soulsby[12] and by Coombs, Pout and Soulsby.[13] These workers showed that both antibody and complement were fixed to the cuticles of certain nematodes. After exposure to antibody, complement, and adherent leucocytes, the cuticle was shown to become increasingly permeable to eosin and methylene blue. This could have obvious deleterious effects upon parasitic nematodes.

Soulsby has presented evidence that hatching fluid and exsheathing fluid, released on hatching of nematode ova and moulting (ecdysis) of larvae may contain functional antigens. This evidence will be discussed below in relation to the self-cure phenomenon. These fluids have been found to contain a variety of enzymes that are probably antigenic.[12,14]

MECHANISMS OF IMMUNITY TO NEMATODES

Humoral Aspects

Taliaferro and Sarles presented evidence for a primary role of serum antibody in immunity to *Nippostrongylus braziliensis* by demonstrating that considerable immunity could be transferred passively to normal rats with serum from actively immunized rats before challenging with infective larvae. Serum antibody was shown by these workers to delay the migrations of larval nematodes, to stunt the growth of the parasites in all stages of development, to decrease the viability of the worms, to decrease ova production, and to accelerate the host's expulsion of the helminths.[2-4]

Rhodes et al reported that immunization of guinea pigs with a purified enzyme from *Ascaris* (i.e., malic dehydrogenase) did appear to offer some protection against challenge infection with this parasite.

These workers provided strong evidence that an antibody directed against a specific parasite enzyme could influence unfavorably the development of the parasite in that host, although it did not prove that such a mechanism was operative in natural infection immunity.[15]

Crandall and Arean investigated the effects of humoral factors in immunity to *Ascaris* by placing second-stage larvae in Millipore diffusion chambers and implanting these chambers intraperitoneally into immune and non-immune mice. These chambers are permeable to host humoral factors, e.g. gamma-globulins, but exclude all host cells. The larvae were found to survive equally well in both immune and non-immune mice, but were observed to grow only in those chambers implanted in normal mice. Larvae whose development was retarded by implantation in immune mice resumed normal development when the chambers were transferred to normal mice.[16]

In a later study, Crandall transferred immunity to *Ascaris* from immune to normal isologous mice by joining them parabiotically.

She was less successful in transferring immunity by immune serum alone, and unsuccessful in transferring immunity by treating normal mice with immune spleen cells and peritoneal exudate cells. These results seem to indicate that both serum and cells are important in functional immunity to *Ascaris*, since parabiosis permits both humoral and cellular components to be shared by both partners.[17]

Cellular Reactions and Hypersensitivities

Among the cells seen in immune responses to nematodes are neutrophiles, eosinophiles, macrophages, mast cells, lymphocytes and plasma-cells. Since many of these cells are involved in various allergic reactions, they will be discussed in connection with hypersensitivity.

Strong evidence exists that animals parasitized by nematodes with a parenteral phase of development become allergically sensitized to the parasites. Immediate-type allergies have been described in trichinosis,[18,19] in cattle lungworm disease,[20] in *Nippostrongylus* infection in the rat,[21] and *Strongyloides* infection in mice.[22] The evidence for immediate types of hypersensitivity occurring in nematode infections may be briefly summarized. Eosinophilia is common, nearly universal, in helminthic disease. Mast cells in the vicinity of migrating parasites can be seen to degranulate. Metachromatic degranulation of mast cells can also be induced by local injection of somatic or metabolic (E.S.) antigens.[18] These hypersensitivity reactions can be to some extent transferred passively. When Briggs injected *Trichinella* antigens into infected mice, he produced anaphylactic reactions. These were evidenced by unsteady gait, decrease in spontaneous activity, prostration, urination, acute dyspnea, cyanosis, convulsive kicking movement, and death within one hour. Some mice also exhibited diarrhea. Uninfected mice showed no such effects upon intravenous injections of antigen, even when the amount injected was increased.[18,19] More recently, Urquhart et al have demonstrated similar anaphylactic reactions with extracts of *Nippostrongylus* in mice passively immunized with serum from actively immune animals. These workers also noted local transudation of Evans Blue-labeled serum when the antigen extracts were injected subcutaneously.[21]

To the author's knowledge, convincing evidence of *delayed*

allergy to nematodes has not been reported. By transferring peritoneal exudate cells from immune donor mice to non-immune recipients of the same species, Larsh and his colleagues observed that the recipients showed an accelerated ability to expel the parasites on challenge infection. The degree of accelerated expulsion of worms appeared to depend on the number of cells transferred. These workers were unable to duplicate their results with lymphnode cells from immune donors. From these data, they postulated that the effects were due to delayed hypersensitivity to the parasite.[23,24] In the author's opinion, their published evidence does not warrant this conclusion for the following reasons. They did not report any assay systems for delayed allergy to *Trichinella* either by the use of a skin test or other means. It is not established that delayed allergy to this nematode even occurs. They did not include an important control, i.e., groups of normal recipients receiving peritoneal exudate cells from non-immune donors. Without this control it is impossible to determine whether the results obtained are due to immune cells. The ability of peritoneal exudates but not lymph-node cells to transfer immunity makes their results appear to be a cellular immunity phenomenon rather than delayed allergy. Peritoneal exudates in the mouse are predominantly composed of macrophages on the third day after injection of mineral oil into the peritoneum. The phenomenon referred to as cellular immunity is mediated by macrophages, while delayed allergy is ordinarily mediated by cells of the lymphocytic series, and should be transferable by grafts of lymph-node cells from sensitized animals. The phenomena reported by Larsh et al appear to be functional immune reactions, rather than hypersensitivity. For further clarification of this point, the reader is referred to a discussion of cellular immunity.[25]

Reactions classified broadly as allergy can lead in some cases to a rapid expulsion of all parasites from the host. Such a phenomenon is termed self-cure, and will be discussed below.

Self-Cure

This phenomenon was initially described for *Haemonchus contortus*, the stomach-worm of sheep, and has recently been reviewed with respect to this parasite by Soulsby.[12,14] It has been described recently for *Nippostrongylus* infection by Urquhart et al[23] and Mulligan et al.[25] Soulsby has discussed experiments that show self-cure reactions in cattle lungworm (*Dictyocaulus*) disease and *Trichostrongylus* infections as well.[12]

The stomach-worm disease of sheep is illustrative of the self-cure phenomenon. The adult worm imbeds itself in that portion of the ruminant stomach known as the abomasum. As long as sheep infected with this parasite are not exposed to reinfection, the condition remains a relatively stable balance between host and parasite. However, if such sheep are challenged with a second dose of infective larvae, self-cure may occur. The abomasum of the animal undergoing self-cure becomes markedly edematous. Histamine levels rise rapidly in the tissues of the abomasum, and later, also in the blood. These reactions apparently render the abomasum an unsuitable environment for parasites in general; all parasites present in the abomasum of the animals undergoing self-cure are expelled, including those that are serologically unrelated to *Haemonchus*. Soulsby and his colleagues showed that the immediate factor that precipitated self-cure was probably the moulting (ecdysis) of the third-stage larvae to fourth-stage larvae; at such times, exsheathing fluid is released. This fluid contains a variety of antigenic constituents.[12]

In the case of *Nippostrongylus* and *Haemonchus* infections, self-cure is of great value to the well-being of the host since it results in the spontaneous elimination of the parasite. However, in *Dictyocaulus* (lungworm) infection of cattle, the self-cure reaction very often has a lethal effect on the host. The animal dies in acute pulmonary edema, which is initiated by the hypersensitive response to the worms in the lungs.[12]

In summary, it will be noted that the self-cure phenomenon bears all of the earmarks of an allergic reaction of the immediate type which is elicited by the parenteral release of helminth antigens during the ecdysis of larvae. The interesting feature of this allergic reaction is that the host may either benefit or be harmed by it, depending upon the location of the parasite and the particular shock tissue. Soulsby has pointed out that self-cure is an important factor in eliminating hemonchiasis of sheep under natural conditions as well as in the laboratory. For this reason, a response showing all of the characteristics of an immediate-type allergy fulfills our definition of a functional immune reaction in certain types of infection.[12]

VACCINATION

Where active immunity to parasites can be demonstrated, there is hope for the development of vaccines to protect against infection. The search for vaccines must take into account the known features of the functional immune response to the parasite; a given type of antigen may be effective in immunizing against one type of parasite and totally ineffective against others that show different types of host-parasite interactions. To illustrate this point, the reader is reminded that simple antigenic exposure to the polysaccharide capsular material of *pneumococcus* confers immunity to infection with the corresponding type of virulent *pneumococcus*, while a living vaccine (e.g., BCG) appears to induce functional immunity to tuberculosis.

Vaccines prepared from somatic antigens of nematodes have generally proven ineffective in conferring functional immunity to these parasites. The reasons for this have been discussed above (Nature of Functional Antigens). Thorson has presented an excellent paper on this subject, to which the reader is referred.[5]

The same considerations that predict the inefficacy of vaccines prepared from ground-up worms also predict that metabolic products might render a vaccine effective.

E.S. antigens, as described above, confer significant immunity to many helminths,[5,10,11,16] and at least one purified enzyme has also been used to accomplish this end.[15] E.S. vaccines, mixtures of enzymes, and larvae in diffusion chambers should be studied in greater detail with a view toward developing effective immunizing agents.[5,10,11,15,16]

A novel method of vaccination that has been tried against *Ascaris* and *Trichinella* is exposing the host to infective larvae followed by specific chemotherapy before the infections reach the more damaging stages. The results of such studies are quite encouraging, and it is hoped that more work along this line will be forthcoming.[26-28]

Another approach is infection with larvae that have been irradiated sufficiently to impair their development in the host, while allowing some metabolism to occur. Such vaccines have been investigated against *Ancylostoma caninum* (a dog hookworm)[29-32] *Nippostrongylus braziliensis*,[33] *Trichinella spiralis*,[34] and *Dictyo-*

caulus viviparous (cattle lungworm).[35] These are highly effective vaccines, but have a very limited shelf-life (measured in hours).

EPILOGUE

The foregoing discussion has endeavored to present the reader with a few concepts that may be involved in immune reactions to nematode infections. It is painfully evident that our understanding of host immunity to these interesting diseases is very rudimentary. In spite of the rapid expansion of immunology as a science, these diseases appear to have been left behind in favor of more accessible systems in the study of immune responses. This is certainly unfortunate in view of the world-wide importance of the nematodes as parasites of man and his domestic animals; insidious, smouldering diseases such as hookworm infestation have crippled the development of entire nations. It is fervently hoped that these relatively neglected systems will be investigated by more immunologists because of their medical and economic importance, as well as their intrinsic interest.

ACKNOWLEDGEMENT

The author wishes to express his deepest gratitude to Dr. C. J. Weinmann, Mr. Robert A. Hyman, and Dr. Reinhard S. Speck for their valuable suggestions in the preparation of this manuscript.

FOOTNOTES

1. Chandler, A. C.: Susceptibility and Resistance to Helminthic Infections. J Parasit 18:135, 1932.
2. Taliaferro, W. H., and Sarles, M. P.: The Cellular Reactions in the Skin, Lungs, and Intestine of Normal and Immune Rats After Infection with *Nippostrongylus muris*. J Infect Dis 64:157, 1939.
3. Taliaferro, W. H.: Immunity to Infections with Parasitic Worms. Physiol Rev 20:469, 1940.
4. Taliaferro, W. H., and Sarles, M. P.: Histopathology of Rats During Passive Immunity to *Nippostrongylus muris*. J Infect Dis 71:69, 1942.
5. Thorson, R. E.: Seminar on Immunity to Parasitic Helminths. II. Physiology of Immunity to Helminth Infections. Exp Parasit 13:3, 1963.

6. Thorson, R. E.: Effect of Immune Serum from Rats on Infective Larvae of *Nippostrongylus muris*. Exp Parasit 3:9, 1954.

7. Thorson, R. E.: Absorption of Protective Antibodies from Serum of Rats Immune to the Nematode, *Nippostrongylus muris*. J Parasit 40:1, 1954.

8. Thorson, R. E.: The Use of "Metabolic" and Somatic Antigens in the Diagnosis of Helminthic Infections. Amer J Hyg Monographic Series No. 22:V, July 1963.

9. Thorson, R. E.: Studies on the Mechanism of Immunity in the Rat to the Nematode, *Nippostrongylus muris*. Amer J Hyg 58:1, 1953.

10. Mills, C. K., and Kent, N. H.: Excretions and Secretions of *Trichinella spiralis* and Their Role in Immunity. Exp Parasit 16:300, 1965.

11. Thorson, R. E.: The Stimulation of Acquired Immunity in Dogs by Injections of Extracts of the Esophagus of Adult Hookworms. J Parasit 42:501, 1956.

12. Soulsby, E. J. L.: Antigen-Antibody Reactions in Helminth Infections. Advance Immunol 2:265, 1962.

13. Coombs, R. R. A., Pout, D. D., and Soulsby, E. J. L.: Globulin, Possibly of Antibody Nature, Combining with the Cuticle of Live *Turbatrix aceti*. Exp Parasit 16:311, 1965.

14. Soulsby, E. J. L.: The Nature and Origin of the Functional Antigens in Helminth Infections. Ann N Y Acad Sci 113:Art 1, 492, 1963.

15. Rhodes, M. B., Nayak, D. P., Kelley, G. W., Jr., and Marsh, C. L.: Studies in Helminth Enzymology. IV. Immune Responses to Malic Dehydrogenase from *Ascaris suum*. Exp Parasit 16:373, 1965.

16. Crandall, C. A., and Arean, V. M.: *In vivo* Studies of *Ascaris suum* Larvae Planted in Diffusion Chambers in Immune and Non-Immune Mice. J Parasit 50:685, 1964.

17. Crandall, C. A.: Studies on the Transfer of Immunity to *Ascaris suum* in Mice by Serum, Parabiotic Union, and Cells. J Parasit 51:405, 1965.

18. Briggs, N. T.: Immunologic Injury to Mast Cells in Mice Actively and Passively Sensitized to Antigens from *Trichinella spiralis*. J Infect Dis 113:22, 1963.

19. Briggs, N. T.: Hypersensitivity in Murine Trichinosis. Ann N Y Acad Sci 113: Art 1, 456, 1963.

20. Weber, T. B., and Rubin, R.: The Eosinophilic Response to Infection with the Lungworm. J Infect Dis 102:214, 1958.

21. Urquhart, G. M., Mulligan, W., Eadie, R. M., and Jennings, F. W.: Immunological Studies on *Nippostrongylus braziliensis* Infection in the Rat: The Role of Local Anaphylaxis. Exp Parasit 17:210, 1965.

22. Goldgraber, M. B., and Lewert, R. M.: Immunological Injury of Mast Cells and Connective Tissues in Mice Infected with *Strongyloides ratti*. J Parasit 51:169, 1965.

23. Larsh, J. E., Jr., Goulson, H. T., and Wetherby, N. F.: Studies on Delayed (Cellular) Hypersensitivity in Mice Infected with *Trichinella spiralis*. II. Transfer of Peritoneal Exudate Cells. J Parasit 50:496, 1964.

24. Larsh, J. E., Jr.: Experimental Trichiniasis. Advance Parasit 1:213, 1963.
25. Gordon, B. L.: The Case for Cytophilic Antibody in Cellular Immunity. Ann Allergy 25:1, 1967.
26. Mulligan, W., Urquhart, G. M., Jennings, F. W., and Neilson, J. T. M.: Immunological Studies on *Nippostrongylus braziliensis* Infection in the Rat: The Self-cure Phenomenon. Exp Parasit 16:341, 1965.
27. Campbell, W. C.: Immunizing Effect of Enteral and Enteral-Parenteral Infections of *Trichinella spiralis* in Mice. J Parasit 51:185, 1965.
28. Denham, D. A.: Immunity to *Trichinella spiralis*. I. The Immunity Produced by Mice to the First Four Days of the Intestinal Phase of the Infection. Parasit 56:323, 1966.
29. Campbell, W. C., and Timinsky, S. F.: Immunizations of Rats Against *Ascaris suum*, by means of Non-pulmonary Larval Infections. J Parasit 51:712, 1965.
30. Miller, T. A.: Effect of X-Irradiation Upon the Infective Larvae of *Ancylostoma caninum* and the Immunogenic Effect in Dogs of a Single Infection with 40-kr-Irradiated Larvae. J Parasit 50:735, 1964.
31. Miller, T. A.: Effect of Route of Administration of Vaccine and Challenge on the Immunogenic Efficiency of Double Vaccination with Irradiated *Ancylostoma caninum* Larvae. J Parasit 51:200, 1965.
32. Miller, T. A.: Persistence of Immunity Following Double Vaccination of Pups with X-Irradiated *Ancylostoma caninum* Larvae. J Parasit 51:705, 1965.
33. Miller, T. A.: Comparison of the Immunogenic Efficiencies of Normal and X-Irradiated *Ancylostoma caninum* Larvae in Dogs. J Parasit 52:512, 1966.
34. Prochazka, Z., and Mulligan, W.: Immunological Studies on *Nippostrongylus braziliensis* Infection in the Rat: Experiments with Irradiated Larvae. Exp Parasit 17:51, 1965.
35. Cabrera, P. B., and Gould, S. E.: Resistance to Trichinosis in Swine Induced by Administration of Irradiated Larvae. J Parasit 50:681, 1964.
36. Lucker, J. T., and Vegas, H. H.: Immunization Against the Cattle Lungworm by Irradiated Larvae. J Parasit 46: Supplement 39, 1960.

THE DOROTHY GORDON MEMORIAL LECTURE

delivered at the Opening Exercises at the

HAHNEMANN MEDICAL COLLEGE OF PHILADELPHIA

1962–1968 "Hahnemann and Rush: A Modern Re-evaluation"
Charles S. Cameron, A.B., M.D., F.A.C.S., Sc.D.
President of the Hahnemann Medical College and Hospital

1963 "Some Paradoxes in Modern Medicine"
Fred Baker Rogers, M.D., M.Sc.
Professor of Preventive Medicine and Epidemiology
Temple School of Medicine

1964 "The Hippocratic Oath"
Max Samter, M.D.
Professor of Medicine
The University of Illinois College of Medicine

1965 "Persisting Medical Problems: A Historical Survey"
Lester Snow King, M.D.
Lecturer in Pathology
The University of Illinois College of Medicine
Senior Editor, Journal of the American Medical Assn.

1966 "The Medical Student as a Scientist: Past and Modern
Impact on the Profession"
John C. Rose, M.D.
Dean
Georgetown University School of Medicine

1967 "The Physicians' Tasks and How to Learn to do Them"
William Dock, M.D.
Chief, Medical Service
Veterans Administration Hospital

1969 "The Medical Student's Dilemma: Yesterday and Today"
Louis Lasagna, M.D.
Professor of Pharmacology
The Johns Hopkins Medical School

1970 "The History of Medical Student Activism"
Edward D. Martin, M.D.
Past President of the Student American Medical Association

1971 "The Family Physician's Role in the History of American
Medicine and Implications for the Future"
Edward J. Kowalewski, M.D.
Past President of the American Academy of General Practice

DEDICATION

"The Living Past"

THESE PAGES ARE AFFECTIONATELY
DEDICATED TO MY MOTHER WHO TAUGHT
ME THAT ANYTHING WORTH DOING IS
WORTH DOING WELL AND TO MY FATHER
WHO INSTILLED IN ME A LOVE OF
LEARNING

Cyrus H. Gordon

My story starts at home. My father, Benjamin L. Gordon (1870-1965), had received his early education in the Talmudic academies of Lithuania. The atmosphere in which he was raised was one where learning was prized for its own sake. There were, of course, ignorant members of the community, but even they looked up to the scholars as the cream of mankind. The students were not motivated by courses and credits nor by examination grades. They went from academy to academy (without transfer credits!) so as to be where they could learn most at the feet of the masters. When they felt they could profit more under another teacher, they moved on to another academy. Their initial reputations as qualified scholars depended on the reputation of the scholar who certified them. Certification was given when a master considered a young scholar ready to function on his own as a master. The curriculum was limited to Hebrew and rabbinic Aramaic texts. Whatever the program lacked in ecumenical breadth, it made up in depth and in dedication to the life of learning. My father came to America at almost the age of twenty at the close of the 1880s, and after learning English and whatever else was then required for entering a professional school in the United States, he started his medical education and graduated as a physician from Jefferson Medical College in Philadelphia in 1896.

In his later years my father wrote his autobiography, so that I do not need to tell his life story or eulogize him here. But I should like to note that he was one of those remarkable Victorian individuals who avoided religious obscurantism on the one hand and scientific dehumanization on the other. He cherished traditional learning in its proper place, as well as modern science in its proper place. As a result, I grew up in a home where ancient texts and modern enlightenment were harmoniously intertwined, without the needless extremism of either the William Jennings Bryan or the Clarence Darrow variety.

Cyrus H. Gordon: Forgotten Scripts, New York, 1968, pp. 135–136.

From various Biblical passages, one can deduce that the ancient Hebrews were well aware of the apothecary's art:

"The Lord spoke unto Moses saying: Take thou also unto thee the chief spices, of flowing myrrh five hundred shekels, and of sweet cinnamon, half so much, even two hundred and fifty, and of cassia, five hundred, after the shekel of the sanctuary, and of olive oil a *hin*. And thou shalt make it a holy anointing oil, a perfume compounded after the art of the perfumer; . . . Take unto thee sweet spices, storax, and onycha, galbanum; sweet spices with pure frankincense; of each shalt there be a light weight, and thou shalt make of it incense, a perfume after the art of the perfumer, seasoned with salt, pure and holy. And thou shalt beat some of it very small, and put it before the testimony of the tent of meeting where I will meet thee; it shall be unto you most holy."

Aside from the drugs, the explicit directions to the compounder is of interest. Among other remedies mentioned is mandrake (*dudaim*), which was considered to possess aphrodisiac properties.

It is natural that among a people who viewed sterility as the greatest misfortune, effort should be made to search for remedies that would promote conception. This drug was efficient for Rachel when all else failed. According to the Biblical narrative, Leah's son found mandrake plants in a field, so he brought them to his mother, Leah. Rachel, who wanted them badly made a deal with Leah to turn over the mandrake in return for Jacob's company. As a result of the bargain, Rachel became impregnated. Mandrake has been praised for its aroma in the "Song of Songs."

Balm of Gilead is mentioned many times in ancient Hebrew works. The hills of Gilead, located in central

Transjordania, were famous for their medicinal herbs.
According to Jeremiah, balm of Gilead (which may or
may not have been a definite compound) was used as a
palliative.

Niter (Hebrew *neter*) is used in parallelism to the
word for soap (*borit*). This indicates that niter as well
as soap was employed as a cleaning agent and surface
antiseptic.

Fruits and saps of certain trees were available, such
as, for example, *tsri* (balsam), *nchoth* (tragacanth), and
lott (laudanum). Certain poisonous roots, characterized
by a bitter taste, are mentioned, such as, for example,
pore, rosh and *v'laanah*; *gofrith* (sulfur) is noted with
reference to the destruction of Sodom.

Oil was employed to dress wounds, bruises, and fester-
ing sores. Wine was employed as a mental depressant:
the daughters of Lot drugged their father with wine until
he was in deep stupor. Pharmaceutical substances were
quite numerous in Biblical days; Jeremiah declares, "In
vain dost thou use many medicines, there is no cure for
thee."

Benjaimn Lee Gordon, M.D.: Medicine throughout Antiquity, Phila.,
1949, pp. 264–265.

CHAPTER 5

Mechanisms and Sites of Action of Antihypertensive Drugs

by

RICHARD F. GORDON, M.D.*

Most antihypertensive agents in contemporary use act, at least in part, by diminishing sympathetic tone and hence vascular resistance. Several agents are believed to act principally at postganglionic sites. The mechanisms of their actions is the subject of this paper. Three general topics will be considered: (1) adrenergic transmission, (2) drug action, and (3) clinical implications. Alpha receptor blocking agents and drugs not considered to act primarily at postganglionic sites will not be discussed.

I. ADRENERGIC TRANSMISSION

In the sympathetic postganglionic fiber the neurohumoral transmitter is primarily norepinephrine, one member of a family of chemical substances known as catecholamines.[1] These substances are of low molecular weight containing a catechol nucleus and an amine group (Fig. 1). In ordinary usage this term is reserved for three substances: dopamine and its metabolic products, norepinephrine and epinephrine. In man these are synthesized in the brain

---

*Richard F. Gordon, M.D. is a Fellow in Cardiology at the Hahnemann Medical College and Hospital.

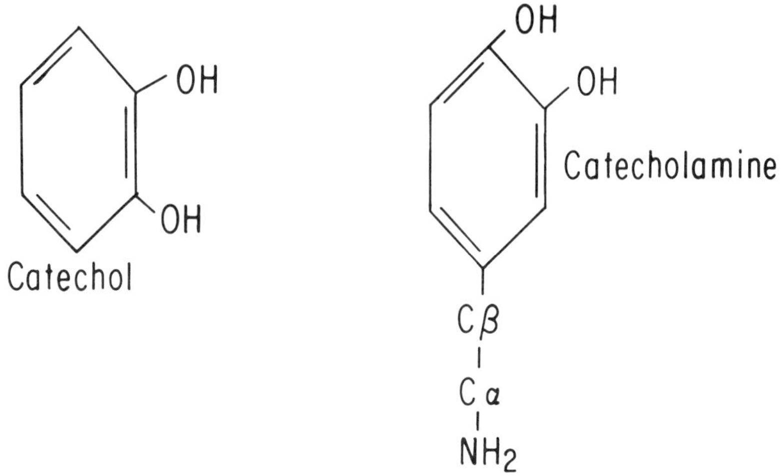

FIG. 1: Basic Catecholamine Structure

and the chromaffin cells of the adrenal medulla as well as in the sympathetic nerve endings, from their precursor tyrosine.

The amino acid tyrosine is present in the intravascular compartment at levels of 10 to 15 micrograms per liter. Presumably, it is taken up in the nerve ending by an active transport mechanism and once inside, undergoes a series of intracellular migrations, from the cytoplasm to the mitochondria, back to the cytoplasm and finally to a specialized subcellular particle, the granulated vesicle. The result of these various steps is the production of norepinephrine (Fig. 2).

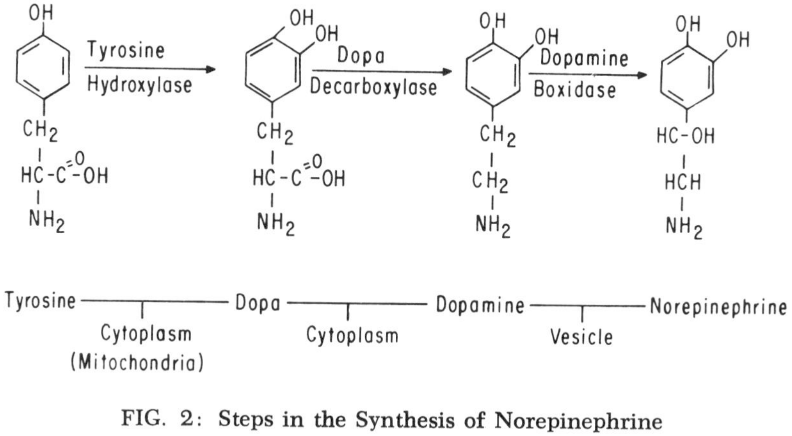

FIG. 2: Steps in the Synthesis of Norepinephrine

In adrenergic nerves almost all of the norepinephrine present in most tissues is located in the granulated vesicles or storage granules.[1,2] The exact mechanism by which it is released from the vesicles in the terminal nerve ending is not definitely known. In 1959 Burn and Rand[3] proposed that acetylcholine played an essential role in such release. This "cholinergic link" hypothesis involves sympathetic impulses releasing acetylcholine, which in turn, acts to alter the permeability of calcium within the nerve ending. Calcium then releases norepinephrine from the granular vesicles (Fig. 3). This theory is supported by Erönkö[4] who has

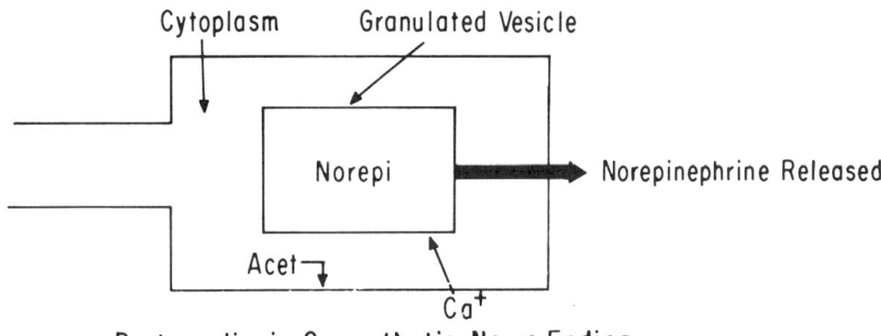

FIG. 3: Schematic Drawing of the "Cholinergic Link" Hypothesis of Catecholamine Release

found that adrenergic fibers in certain tissues stain positively for cholinesterase. Also, it has been found that anticholinesterase drugs such as physostigmine potentiate responses to postganglionic sympathetic nerve stimulation.[5] Additional studies by others have also lent considerable support for this hypothesis.[3,4,5,6,7,8,9] Although this concept is not entirely accepted by all investigators[10] no other more tenable proposal has been suggested at present.

The next concern is the fate of the neurotransmitter after its release from the nerve ending into the blood stream. Ferry[11] found that when norepinephrine was administered to experimental animals sixty percent was found to be taken up by the nerve ending, fifteen percent was disposed of by the enzyme catechol-o-methyltransferase (COMT), five percent was taken up by receptors and acceptors and twenty percent resulted in an overflow into the circulation. Thus, only five percent was involved in end organ response or vascular reactivity (Fig. 4).

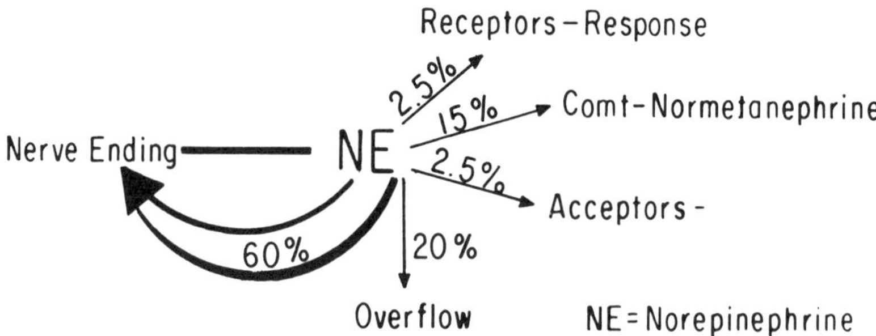

FIG. 4: Distribution of Norepinephrine after Release from Bloodstream (from Ferry, C. B.: The Autonomic Nervous System. *Annual Review of Pharmacology*, Vol. 7, 1967, p. 191.)

Interestingly, like so many other biochemical systems utilizing a negative feedback mechanism, the synthesis of norepinephrine has been recently proposed to be regulated by the concentration of intraneuronal cytoplasmic catecholamine. With a rise in the concentration of norepinephrine, the conversion of tyrosine to dopa is inhibited and thus a negative feedback mechanism may exist at the tyrosine hydroxylase step.[12,13,14]

It has been found that two active transport mechanisms are involved in the neuronal uptake step (sixty percent). The first step occurs at the outer cytoplasmic membrane and the second at the granular membrane; a two-hundred fold concentration gradient exists from cytoplasm to granule[1] (Fig. 5).

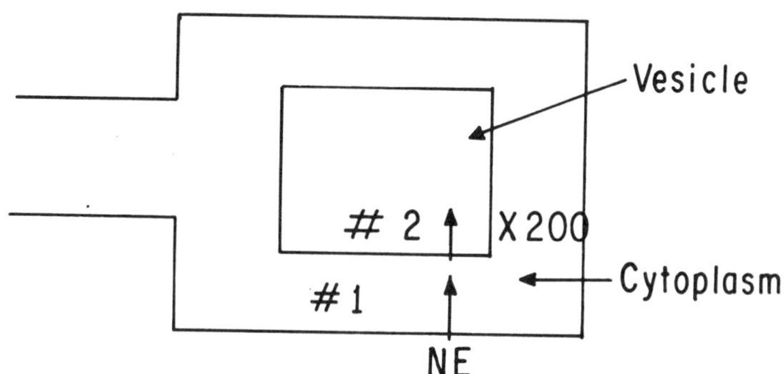

FIG. 5: Schematic Drawing of the Active Uptake of Norepinephrine into the Sympathetic Nerve Ending: Steps #1 and #2

The norepinephrine referred to above commonly has been called the "free" or "liberated" form. In addition, a second type or "stored" norepinephrine has been proposed.[1,14,15,16,17] Here the enzyme monamine oxidase (MAO) and not catechol-o-methyltransferase (COMT) is involved in the amine's metabolism. This enzyme has no apparent role in the physiologic inactivation of circulating neurotransmitter but metabolizes the stored component. It is believed to exist within the mitochondria.[1,14,15,16,17]

Thus, two catecholamine pools have been proposed designated Pool I and Pool II.[1,14,15,16,17] The first, characterized by a rapid turnover, metabolism by COMT and an active release by tyramine, functions as the sympathetic neurohumor. The second, characterized by a slow turnover, metabolism by MAO and no active release by tyramine, functions only as a reserve component. Although both pools are thought to exist in the granulated vesicles, they have not been separated anatomically at the present time (Fig. 6).

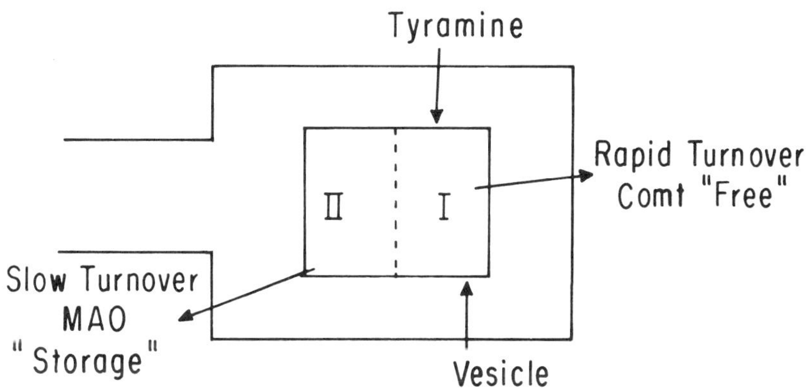

FIG. 6: Schematic Drawing of the Two Postulated Catecholamine Pools (I and II)

II. DRUG ACTION

For purposes of simplification, this discussion of drug action will be divided into those drugs acting at sites of catecholamine syn-

thesis, storage and release and those acting as "false neurotransmitters."

A. Synthesis

One approach to the therapy of hypertension has consisted of
attempts to block the biosynthesis of norepinephrine by the use of
compounds that inhibit the various enzymes involved. Levitt[19]
proposed that the rate limiting step in the biosynthesis of norepinephrine is the conversion of tyrosine to dopa by the enzyme
tyrosine hydroxylase. Spector[20] has shown that alpha-methyl-
tyrosine, a potent inhibitor of tyrosine-hydroxylase, does lower
endogenous levels of norepinephrine by about seventy percent.
The mechanism of lowering is consistent with blockade of the
enzymatic synthesis of norepinephrine at the tyrosine hydroxylase
step.[20] It has further been shown that the action of alpha-methyl-

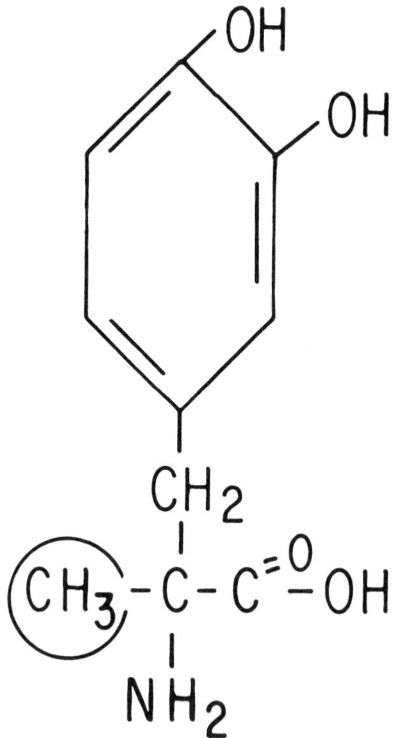

FIG. 7: **Structure of Methyldopa (Aldomet®)**

tyrosine is due to the drug itself and not due to its metabolic products.[21]

Presently, alpha-methyl-tyrosine is used primarily in the treatment of pheochromocytoma.[22] That it works effectively in this but not in essential hypertension substantiates the claim that increased catecholamine synthesis is not the basic problem in the latter disease.[13,23]

Alpha-methyldopa (Aldomet®) is a hypotensive agent now in wide clinical use (Fig. 7). Although a less potent antihypertensive than the ganglionic blocking drugs or guanethidine, it is more potent than reserpine or the thiazide diuretics.[24] It has been shown to inhibit dopa decarboxylase *in vivo*, both in animals and man.[24] But Levine and associates[25] have shown that decarboxylase inactivation does not decrease tissue norepinephrine levels. Further, Muscholl[26] has pointed out that decarboxylase inhibitors more potent than alpha-methyldopa, such as alpha-methyldopa hydrazine, do not lower the blood pressure of hypertensive patients. Thus generally it is felt that alpha-methyldopa acts not by inhibiting the synthesis of norepinephrine but as a "false neurotransmitter," a topic to be discussed further. [24,25,26]

B. Storage

Reserpine, a hypotensive agent used clinically for many years, has proven to be of definite value particularly in the treatment of hypertensive crises. It is generally believed to act by blockade of the active uptake of catecholamine from the cytoplasm to the granulated vesicle of the terminal nerve ending, leading to depletion and enzymatic deamination by monamine oxidase[13,27] (Fig. 8). Since active uptake accounts for the major disposition of circulating catecholamine it is easy to see how interference with this process could lead to a significant depletion of catecholamine and the hypotensive effects clinically observed.

Reserpine, then affects primarily a surplus reserve pool of stored amine. This action of reserpine on the storage mechanism of the granule is irreversible. Recovery is primarily due to a continuous transport down the nerve ending of newly formed amine granules.[17] These may be of importance in the early functional recovery after reserpine administration, since recovery occurs long before tissue stores are repleted.[9]

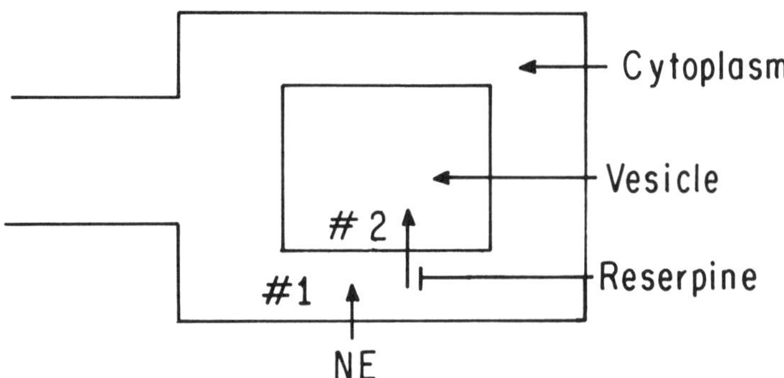

FIG. 8: Schematic Drawing Depicting the Blockade of Norepinephrine Uptake by Reserpine

In addition to the two catecholamine pools (Pools I and II) to which reference has already been made, two additional pools have been proposed which are distinguished primarily by their sensitivity to reserpine. The first is characterized by an $ATP\text{-}mg^{+2}$ dependent reserpine sensitive uptake mechanism; the second by a reserpine resistant uptake mechanism.[14,17,27] The latter is supposed to operate at a norepinephrine concentration of $10^{-4}m$ but not at a concentration of $10^{-5}m$.[14] It has been shown that ^3H aramine is first taken up by a reserpine resistant pool of granules and then is transferred to a reserpine sensitive pool.[17]

Guanethidine (Ismelin®), a guanidine derivative (essentially a two carbon chain separating a ring system from a guanidine group) (Fig. 9) has been shown to **lack the** central action of

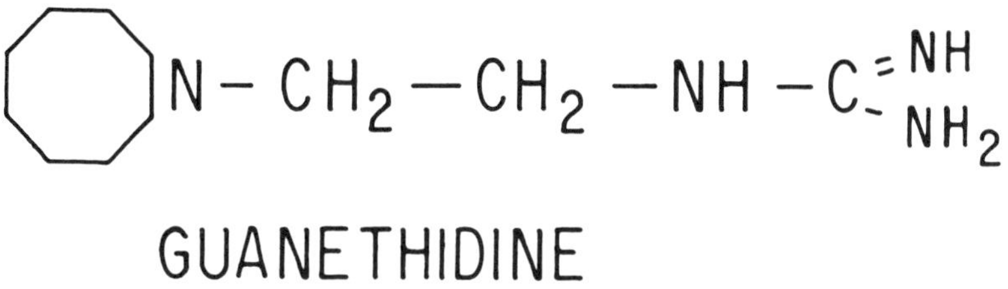

GUANETHIDINE

FIG. 9: Structure of Guanethidine

reserpine and has not been subject to the rapid tolerance development that limits the usefulness of other agents.[28] It is believed to act primarily by the active release of norepinephrine from the granulated vesicle, leading to a transient sympathomimetic effect followed by a total depletion of the reserve pool.[24,29] (Fig. 10).

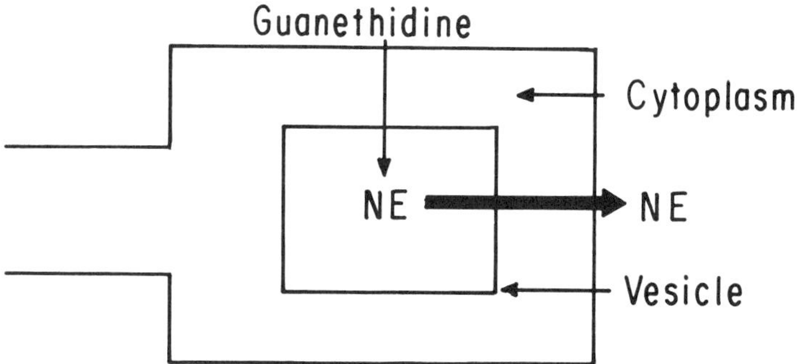

FIG. 10: Schematic Drawing Depicting the Active Release of Norepinephrine by Guanethidine

An alternate explanation for the action of guanethidine involves interference with the "cholinergic link" mechanism of Burn and Rand.[5,9,30]

The guanidine group of guanethidine is strongly basic and highly ionized and similar to the trimethylammonium group of acetylcholine[5] (Fig. 11). It is felt by some[5,9,30] that because of this,

$$(CH_3)_3 \equiv N^+ \cdot CH_2 \cdot CH_2 \cdot O \cdot COCH_3$$

FIG. 11: Structure of Acetylcholine

guanethidine may act as a competitive inhibitor of acetylcholine in interfering with release of catecholamine.

Bethanidine sulfate is another agent believed to influence storage of catecholamine. It is similar to guanethidine but has a shorter onset of action as well as a shorter duration.[29]

Other agents have also been proposed to influence catecholamine storage but these either do not primarily use the storage sites in their mode of activity or have not proven to be clinically useful as hypotensive agents. Chlorpromazine and imipramine, primarily psychotropic agents, have been shown to block the active transport of catecholamine from cytoplasm to granulated vesicles. What this means in relation to the psychotropic effects that these drugs exhibit is not definitely known.

C. Release

Bretylium, a quarternary ammonium compound, may be the prototype of hypotensive agents affecting release of catecholamine[2] (Fig. 12). Rapid tolerance has limited the usefulness of this

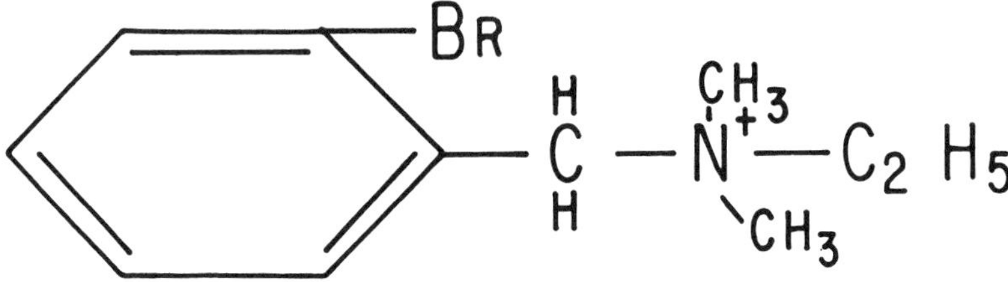

FIG. 12: Structure of Bretylium

drug.[24] Although the general opinion is that bretylium directly prevents nerve impulses from releasing catecholamine at the nerve ending,[2,24,32] other explanations have been offered. Burn and Froede[34] and others[3,5,9,30] have proposed that bretylium like guanethidine is related to acetylcholine in structure and acts by interfering with the "cholinergic link" mechanism.

D. False Neurotransmitters

This term refers to substances not normally present in significant amounts in sympathetic postganglionic nerve endings which replace norepinephrine and are released with resulting decreased vascular tone. It has been shown that alpha-methyldopa is converted into alpha methyl norepinephrine by decarboxlylation and subsequent oxidation; dopa decarboxylase and dopamine-beta-oxidase being the enzymes involved[1,4,13,24,25,26,33,35,36] (Fig. 13). It

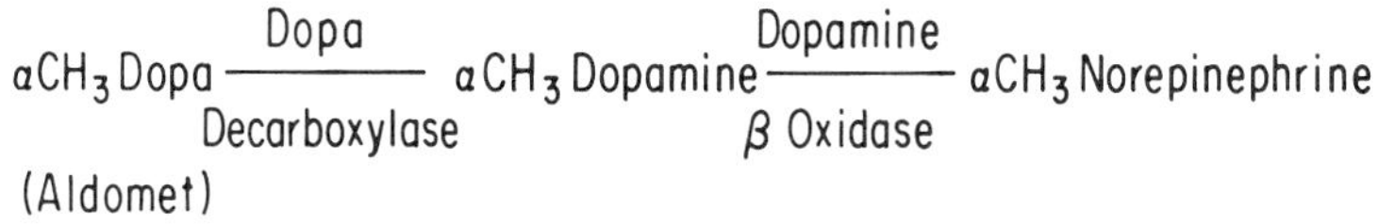

$$\alpha CH_3\,Dopa \xrightarrow[\text{Decarboxylase}]{\text{Dopa}} \alpha CH_3\,Dopamine \xrightarrow[\beta\ \text{Oxidase}]{\text{Dopamine}} \alpha CH_3\,Norepinephrine$$

(Aldomet)

FIG. 13: Synthesis of Alpha Methyl Norepinephrine from Methyldopa (Aldomet®), a "False Neurotransmitter"

has been proposed that the alpha methyl norepinephrine released exerts a weaker action than the norepinephrine at receptor sites and thus a decrease in the effect of sympathetic nerve stimulation occurs.[4,12,24,25,26,33,36] Many investigators have explained the hypotensive action of alpha-methyldopa by this mechanism and not by inhibition of dopa decarboxylase.[12,24,25,26]

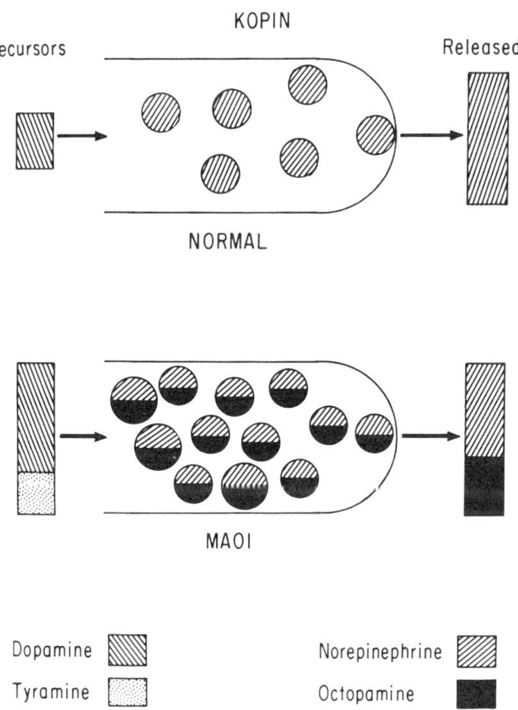

FIG. 14: Schematic Drawing Depicting the Decreased Norepinephrine Release Following the Use of MAO Inhibitors (from Kopin, I. J.; Fischer, J. E.; Musacchio, J. M.; Horst, W. D. and Weise, V. K.: False neurochemical transmitters and the mechanism of sympathetic blockade by monoamine oxidase inhibitors, *J. Pharmacol. Exp. Ther.* 147(2):186–193, 1965.)

The antihypertensive action of monamine oxidase inhibitors such as pargyline also has been explained by many[12,24,33] as an example of false neurotransmission. Kopin[12,33] demonstrated that following monamine oxidase inhibition, endogenously formed amines which can function as false neurotransmitters accumulate in the sympathetic nerves. These endogenously formed amines or phenolic amines are apparently derived from amino acids by the action of amino acid decarboxylase and in some cases dopamine-beta-oxidase. Such compounds as tyramine and octopamine are usually detected in normal urine in only trace amounts. However, there is a marked increase in their excretion when monamine oxidase inhibitors are employed; that is, monamine oxidase inhibition prevents destruction of these substances produced in other tissues and these amines then may replace norepinephrine in storage vesicles. Replacement of norepinephrine by a relatively inactive substitute results in a diminished release of norepinephrine and, therefore, apparent adrenergic blockade[12,33] (Fig. 14).

Also, Kopin[12] has proposed that with displacement of norepinephrine from its binding sites, the blood level of free norepinephrine increases, albeit transiently. During this period, the synthesis of additional catecholamine decreases by way of the negative feedback mechanism referred to previously.[12,13,14] The combination

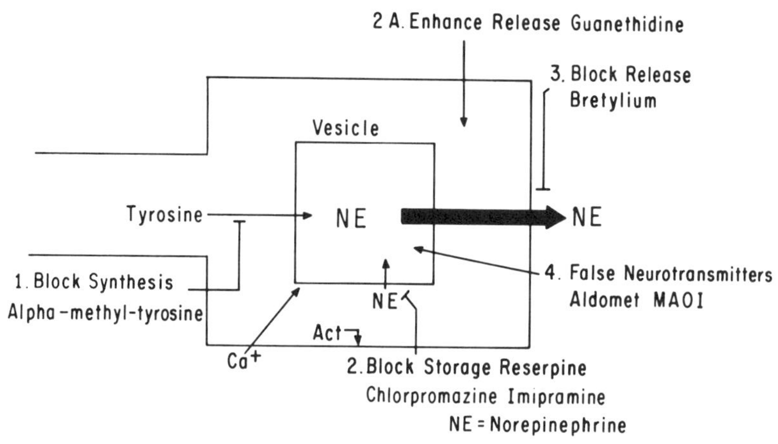

FIG. 15: **Composite of the Sites of Action of Various Antihypertensive Drugs**

then of replacement of active catecholamine by a less potent analogue and of interference of synthesis by a negative feedback system appears to be the explanation for the adrenergic blockade observed with monamine oxidase inhibitors. Central stimulation and orthostatic hypotension have been serious drawbacks in their use today as hypotensive therapeutic agents.[24]

Figure 15 represents a composite of the sites of action of various antihypertensive drugs.

III. CLINICAL IMPLICATIONS

A brief discussion of some of the current antihypertensive therapeutic agents and their mechanisms of action has been presented. The clinical implications are many and varied but a few of the most obvious should be noted.

(1) Reserpine, guanethidine, chlorpromazine, and imipramine are contraindicated in the setting of a pheochromocytoma. The transient sympathomimesis resulting from a blockade of uptake or enhanced release of norepinephrine may lead to a hypertensive crisis. Conversely, if a hypertensive responds to reserpine, the existence of a pheochromocytoma is unlikely.

(2) Chang[37] has proposed that amphetamines compete with guanethidine for active sites on the neuronal membrane and thus antagonize the latter's activity. Since amphetamines are commonly given for obesity due to their anorectic qualities, this proposal should be kept in mind if obesity and hypertension are to be treated at the same time. Conversely, hypotension induced by guanethidine might be reversed by the addition of amphetamines.[38]

(3) Bretylium and guanethidine probably should not be used together since bretylium is thought to act by inhibiting and guanethidine by enhancing the release of norepinephrine.

(4) Similarly, from a theoretical standpoint at least, the combination of reserpine and guanethidine is not ideal because both agents may compete for the same receptor sites.[37] Alpha-methyldopa, on the other hand, acting as a false neurotransmitter, may be quite effective in combination with either of the above two agents.

(5) The use of thiazides and/or hydralazine with the other agents mentioned may be quite effective. These two drugs do not

have a major effect in synthesis, storage or release of norepineph-rine but instead probably have a direct effect on the smooth muscle of the vasculature.[24]

(6) It is generally believed unnecessary to discontinue reserpine prior to elective surgery. The pressor response in this situation appears to be unaffected. Perhaps with the stress of surgery and increase in catecholamine release the reserpine resistant uptake mechanism previously referred to[14,17,27] predominates with no significant depletion in catecholamine stores. Guanethidine and alpha-methyldopa, on the other hand, probably should be dis-continued prior to surgery.[39]

SYNOPSIS—ABSTRACT

The neurohumoral transmitter of the sympathetic postganglionic fiber is primarily norepinephrine. Several antihypertensive agents work by affecting the synthesis, storage or release of this trans-mitter. A fourth group known as "false neurotransmitters" work by replacing norepinephrine in the granulated vesicle of the ter-minal nerve ending. In order to obtain the fullest benefits from medical therapy a precise knowledge of the mechanisms by which the various antihypertensive drugs work is mandatory.

Indexing Terms:
  Hypertension
  Catecholamine
  False neurotransmitters
  Autonomic nervous system
The following abbreviations have been used:
  dopa, 3,4-dihydroxyphenylalanine;
  dopamine, 3,4-dihydroxyphenethylamine;
  alpha-methyldopa, alpha-methyl, 3, 4-dihydroxyphenyalanine

Generic and Trade Names of Drugs
  1. Alpha-methyldopa—Aldomet®
  2. Benzothiadiazine (thiazide)—Diuril®, etc.
  3. Bretylium tosylate—Darenthin®
  4. Chlorpromazine—Thorazine®
  5. Guanethidine sulfate—Ismelin®
  6. Hydralazine hydrochloride—Apresoline hydrochloride®

7. Imipramine hydrochloride—Tofranil®
8. Pargyline hydrochloride—Eutonyl®
9. Phenoxybenzamine hydrochloride—Dibenzyline®
10. Reserpine—Serpasil®, etc.

FOOTNOTES

1. Wurtman, R. J.: Catecholamines, *New Eng. J. Med.* 273:637–645; 693–699; 746–753, 1965.

2. Brodie, B. B.: Recent views on mechanisms for lowering sympathetic tone, *Circulation* 28:970–986, 1963.

3. Burn, J. H., Rand, M. J.: Acetylcholine in adrenergic transmission, *Ann. Rev. Pharmacol.* 5:163–182, 1965.

4. Erönkö, O.: Histochemistry of nervous tissues: catecholamines and cholinesterases, *Ann. Rev. Pharmacol.* 7:203–222, 1967.

5. Arya, P. C.: Cholinergic link hypothesis and sympathetic transmission at the nictitating membrane of the dog, *Brit. J. Pharmacol.* 33:413–425, 1968.

6. Burn, J. H., Froede, E.: The action of substances which block sympathetic postganglionic nervous transmission, *Brit. J. Pharmacol.* 20: 378–387, 1963.

7. Burn, J. H., Gibbons, W. R.: The sympathetic postganglionic fibre and the block by bretylium; the block prevented by hexamethonium and initiated by mecamylamine, *Brit. J. Pharmacol.* 22(3):549–557, 1964.

8. McGiff, J. C., Burns, R. B. P., Blumenthal, M. R.: Role of acetylcholine in the renal vasoconstrictor response to sympathetic nerve stimulation in the dog, *Circulation Res.* 20:616–629, 1967.

9. Kopin, I. J.: Acetylcholine, bretylium and release of norepinephrine from the sympathetic nerve ending. *Ann. N. Y. Acad. Sci.* 144:558–562; 563–570, 1967.

10. Burnstock, G., Robinson, P.M.: Localization of catecholamines and acetylcholinesterase in autonomic nerves. *Circulation Res.* 21:Suppl. 3: 43–55, 1967.

11. Ferry, C. B.: The autonomic nervous system. *Ann. Rev. Pharmacol.* 7:185–202, 1967.

12. Kopin, I. J.: False adrenergic transmitters. *Ann. Rev. Pharmacol.* 8:377–394, 1968.

13. Bloom, F. E., Giarman, N. J.: Physiologic and pharmacologic considerations of biogenic amines in the nervous system. *Ann. Rev. Pharmacol.* 8:229–258, 1968.

14. Von Euler, U. S.: Some factors affecting catecholamine uptake, storage, and release in adrenergic nerve granules. *Circulation Res.* 21: Suppl. 3:5–11, 1967.

15. Braunwald, E., Chidsey, C. A., Harrison, D. C., *et al.*: Studies on the function of the adrenergic nerve endings in the heart. *Circulation* 28: 956–969, 1963.

16. Kopin, I. J.: Storage and metabolism of catecholamines. The role of monamine oxidase. *Pharmacol. Rev.* 16:179–191, 1964.

17. Andren, N. E.: Adrenergic mechanisms. *Ann. Rev. Pharmacol.* 9: 119–134, 1969.

18. Von Euler, U. S., Lishajko, F.: Mechanism of drug-induced catecholamine release from adrenergic nerve granules. *Circulation Res.* 21: Suppl. 3:63–69, 1967.

19. Levitt, M., Spector, S., Sjoerdsma, A., *et al.*: Elucidation of the rate-limiting step in norepinephrine biosynthesis in the perfused guinea-pig heart. *J. Pharmacol. Exp. Ther.* 148(1):1–8, 1965.

20. Spector, S., Sjoerdsma, A., Udenfriend, S.: Blockade of endogenous norepinephrine synthesis by alpha-methyl-tyrosine, an inhibitor of tyrosine hydroxylase. *J. Pharmacol. Exp. Ther.* 147(1):86–95, 1965.

21. Engelman, K., Jéquier, E., Udenfriend, S., *et al.*: Metabolism of alpha-methyltyrosine in man: relationship to its potency as an inhibitor of catecholamine biosynthesis. *J. Clin. Invest.* 47:568–576, 1968.

22. Engelman, K., Horwitz, D., Jéquier, E., *et al.*: Biochemical and pharmacologic effects of alpha-methyltyrosine in man. *J. Clin. Invest.* 47: 577–594, 1968.

23. Mendlowitz, M., Wolf, R. L., Gitlow, S. E.: Catecholamine metabolism in essential hypertension. *Amer. Heart J.* 79(3):401–405, 1970.

24. Pardo, E. G., Vargos, R., Vidrio, H.: Antihypertensive drug action. *Ann. Rev. Pharmacol.* 5:77–98, 1965.

25. Levine, R. J., Sjoerdsma, A.: Dissociation of the decarboxylase-inhibiting and norepinephrine-depleting effects of alpha-methyldopa, alpha-ethyl-dopa, 4-bromo-3 hydroxy-benzyloxyamine and related substances. *J. Pharmacol. Exp. Ther.* 146:42–47, 1964.

26. Muscholl, E.: Autonomic nervous system: newer mechanisms of adrenergic blockade. *Ann. Rev. Pharmacol.* 6:107–128, 1966.

27. Malmfors, T.: Fluorescent histochemical studies on the uptake, storage and release of catecholamines. *Circulation Res.* 21:Suppl. 3:25–42, 1967.

28. Green, A. F., Robson, R. L.: Comparison of the effects of bretylium guanethidine and bethanidine on smooth muscle responses to different rates of sympathetic nerve stimulation. *Brit. J. Pharmacol.* 22:349–355, 1964.

29. Moser, M.: Guanethidine and bethanidine in the management of hypertension. *Amer. Heart J.* 77: 426–436, 1969.

30. Rand, M. J., Wilson, J.: Receptor site of adrenergic neuron blocking drugs. *Circulation Res.* 21:Suppl. 3:89–99, 1967.

31. Brodie, B. B.: Recent views on mechanisms for lowering sympathetic tone. *Circulation* 28:970–986, 1963.

32. Burnstock, G., Holman, M. E.: Effect of drugs on smooth muscle. *Ann. Rev. Pharmacol.* 6:129–156, 1966.

33. Kopin, I. J., Fisher, J. E., Musacchio, J. M., *et al.*: "False neuro-chemical transmitters" and the mechanism of sympathetic blockade by monamine oxidase inhibitors. *J. Pharmacol. Exp. Ther.* 147(2):186–193, 1965.

34. Burn, J. H., Froede, H.: The action of substances which block sympathetic postganglionic nervous transmission. *Brit. J. Pharmacol.* 20: 378–387, 1963.

35. Brunner, H., Hedwall, P. R., Maitre, L., Meier, M.: Antihypertensive effects of alpha-methylated catecholamine analogues in the rat. *Brit. J. Pharmacol.* 30:108–122, 1967.

36. Shore, P. A., Busfield, D., Alpers, H. S.: Binding and release of metaraminol: mechanism of norepinephrine depletion by alpha-methyl-m-tyrosine and related agents. *J. Pharmacol. Exp. Ther.* 146(2):194–199, 1964.

37. Chang, C. C., Costa, E., Brodie, B. B.: Interaction of guanethidine with adrenergic neurons. *J. Pharmacol. Exp. Ther.* 147(3):303–312, 1965.

38. Harvey, S. C., *et al.*: Effects of amphetamines on plasma catecholamines. *Arch. Int. Pharmacodym.* 172:301–322, 1968.

39. Dingle, H. R.: Antihypertensive drugs and anaesthesia. *Anaesthesia* 21:151–172, 1966.

DEDICATION

"The Common Background of Greek and Hebrew Civilization"

DEDICATED TO MY FATHER

BENJAMIN LEE GORDON

PHYSICIAN AND HEBRAIST

WHO TAUGHT ME TO CHERISH ANCIENT TRADITION

AS WELL AS MODERN ENLIGHTENMENT

Cyrus H. Gordon

THE DOCTOR BENJAMIN LEE
AND
DOROTHY GORDON MEMORIAL SCHOLARSHIP

The Dr. Benjamin Lee and Dorothy Gordon Memorial Scholarship is unique in various aspects. The scholarship consists of $5,000 which is awarded to one Atlantic County individual (male or female) on the basis of a combination of financial need and academic merit to enable the recipient to afford a complete medical education.

The scholarship is an outright gift free of all strings and encumbrances. The $5,000 is divided into four yearly stipends. The recipient undertakes no indebtedness and no repayment is permitted. The scope of his future practice remains entirely at his own discretion.

The scholarship is awarded yearly by the Scholarship Committee of the Atlantic County Medical Society and is administered by the Atlantic County Medical Society.

Maurice Bear Gordon, M.D.: The What and Why of the Gordon Medical Scholarship Program, *Medical Times*, Vol. 98, No. 10, October 1970, p. 100.

The Loango and Kakango natives of West Africa believe that some diseases are due to human agencies such as witchcraft and the evil eye; others are due to evil spirits. The great morbidity and mortality from smallpox and sleeping sickness, and for that matter all diseases that take on an epidemic form, they regard as a scourge sent by some outraged nature spirit. They hold the demon of smallpox in such dread that they have a repugnance even to the mention of his name. The cholera demon, called *rak*, is said to haunt the abodes of man whom he afflicts with pain in the stomach and head. These demons are exorcised by means of a dance, during which magic formulae are chanted by the magician.

On the West Coast of Africa, when the *Abiku* (evil spirit attacking children) takes possession of a child it is believed that he allocates for himself the greater part of food given to the child. Consequently the child becomes emaciated and pines away. When a child is irritable and cries more than usual, it is thought that he is being hurt by the *Abiku*. The anxious mother offers a sacrifice of food, and while the attention of the *Abiku* is diverted to the devouring of the food, the mother attaches anklets made from iron necklaces to the child. The jingling of the iron when the child walks is supposed to chase the *Abiku* away. If no improvement takes place, the mother tries to cast out the possessing *Abiku* by making small incisions in the body of the child, and dusting these with pepper, believing that she will thereby cause pain to the *Abiku* within and make him depart. Since everything done to the child is felt by the Abiku, the screaming of the child with pain is amply compensated by the belief that the *Abiku* is also suffering.

Benjamin Lee Gordon, M.D.: The Romance of Medicine, Phila., 1944, pp. 7–8.

CHAPTER 6

Concepts of Nagual as a Means of Social Control in the Tzeltal and Tzotzil Communities of Chiapas, Mexico

by

RACHEL K. GORDON*

Originally it was the author's purpose to investigate the single concept of animal-spirit-companion labeled *"nagual."* Evaluation of the ethnographic reports of various anthropologists concerning diverse Tzeltal and Tzotzil communities demonstrated that this task was impossible for two reasons: In the first place, the term *"nagual,"* being a Nahuatl word, is never found in those villages where it has several other names. In Zinacantan the animal-spirit-companion is called "chanul"; in San Pedro Chenalhó, "Wayhel"; in Chamula, "chulel," etc. Secondly, far from denoting a single concept, *nagual* is the basis of a whole set of religious beliefs focusing on the ancestral deities. The exact definition of *nagual* and the related beliefs vary in their details from community to community.

Nonetheless, throughout the region of Chiapas, Mexico, the beliefs relating to *nagual* and corresponding practices provide means of social control or ways of maintaining traditional, co-operative relations among the members of a community. Numer-

---

*Rachel K. Gordon is an undergraduate student at Brandeis University.

ous ceremonies are structured according to these beliefs, and these ceremonies help to maintain the traditional social order, a concept to be later developed.

Reference to *nagual*, then in this study is solely for the sake of simplicity. Let us proceed to analyze these beliefs in detail.

Throughout Chiapas it is believed that every man or at least every member of one's community, has an animal-spirit-companion as his counterpart. It is a natural, wild animal which has the same soul as the person. A man shares the lifespan of his *nagual*, so that if the *nagual* dies, so does he, and vice-versa.

The relationship also extends to particulars. If the *nagual* is fat and satisfied, the person is healthy; if it cannot find food, the person will go hungry. The individual and his *nagual* have a single personality. Actions of the individual affect the life of his *chulel*, which then has repercussions in the individual's life.[1] The above description of the concept of *nagual* is fairly general, but it is employed because Pozas has found it to be true for Chamula. Since Pozas has not paid much attention to the concept, his description of it is incomplete. Sketchy as it is, however, it serves to define the concept.

Guiteras-Holmes has gone farther in describing the interdependence of the individual and his *nagual* as conceived in San Pedro Chenalhó, and her findings agree with those of Pozas closely enough for us to infer that they are true for Chamula and many other communities. A *nagual* may be related to one of thirteen evil powers "above," in which case it is referred to as "poslob" meaning "jaguar"; or it may be related to one of the powers from "below" which are not necessarily evil.[2]

The qualities of a *nagual* reflect the personality and temperament of its human counterpart. The jaguar and hummingbird respectively represent the extremely "evil" and extremely "good" personality types. Thus, he who possesses a jaguar for *nagual* is "capricho": willful, stubborn, hot-tempered and heedless while the possessor of a hummingbird *nagual* is "humilde": patient, understanding, sweet-tempered and considerate. Despite these differences, all *naguals* can cause harm and are to be feared.[3]

Yet a man controls his own fate: by "good conduct," (i.e., traditional behavior) he can insure his continued existence;[4] while through "bad conduct" (i.e., behavior contrary to tradition) he will bring about his own destruction. The hummingbird is distinguished from other *naguals* in that it harms the others only as punishment for the sins of their owners for its primary role is to care for all good *naguals*.[3]

Vogt and Holland describe the concepts of *nagual* in Larrainzar and Zinacantan much more specifically. The members of both communities conceive of a series of supernatural corrals containing the animal-spirit-companion of each community member. Separate corrals house jaguars, coyotes, ocelots and smaller animals. The *naguals* are cared for by the ancestral gods. Each day they are let out of the corrals and transformed into cows and sheep so that they may graze, and in the evening they are herded back into their corrals for safety. Once back in the corrals, where they can no longer harm other animals or be harmed, they are converted back into their previous wild animal forms.[5]

The ancestral gods are crucial, for they have complete control over the *naguals*. It is they who install a single soul into the embryo of a person and the embryo of an animal, thus linking their life-spans.[6] It is they who care for the animal throughout its life and, therefore, for the person. They may choose to neglect the animal and leave it to wander in the forest at night,[5] and if they do so it will certainly be harmed for, as Guiteras-Holmes has pointed out, the forest at night is filled with evil spirits who seek the destruction of man.[4] Thus, it is necessary always to please the ancestral gods, for they are responsible for human welfare. Vogt has pointed out that the ancestral gods are the most important deities in all Tzeltal and Tzotzil villages[7] and it is reasonable to infer from this fact and from the widespread belief in *naguals* that the ancestral gods are everywhere believed to care for the animal-spirit-companions of their human descendants. Ceremonies honoring the ancestral gods insure that they will take care of the *naguals* and, by extension, the Indians. In this way, all ceremonies honoring the ancestral gods are based on the *nagual* concept.

In all Tzotzil and Tzeltal communities, crosses and rituals associated with them represent the various units and levels of the social structure. The family has its own cross-shrine in its courtyard; the localized lineages and waterhole groups have one on a more distant hill; and the entire community has one on at least one sacred mountain with a shrine.[8] Rituals at a cross-shrine are a means of communicating with the ancestral gods. The animal-spirit-companions dwelling in the corrals in the sacred mountains maintain the same social and familial relations as do their human counterparts.[9] Thus, when groups of people get together to honor the ancestral gods, they believe that their *naguals* are also in harmony with one another. At each "Kalvario," or cross-shrine representing a large social unit, a particular group of ancestral gods is believed to meet to deliberate about the affairs of their living descendants and to await offerings.[10]

In Zinacantan, each localized patrilineage clarifies its boundaries and composition by its own annual K'in Krus ceremony. This elaborate ceremony opens with a ritual meal in the house of the senior majordomo; at the end of the meal the shamans of the lineage recite a long prayer; then comes an all-night ceremonial circuit around the lineage's lands, including a visit to each cross-shrine so that lineage members may place flowers and offerings there and pray to the ancestral deities. A second ritual meal closes the K'in Krus ceremony.[11] The ceremony symbolizes the unity of the lineage and the rights of its members to their inherited lands, honors the ancestral gods who care for the *naguals*, and links their human counterparts who have come together to worship.[12] Water-hole groups, consisting of from two to thirteen patrilineal clans also have a K'in Krus ceremony, which expresses their right to use the waterhole and links together the member lineage groups.

All ceremonies in Zinacantan are modeled after the Zinacantecos' conception of the ancestral gods as guardians of the *naguals*. The ancestral gods are believed to "embrace" the eight hundred companion animal-spirits of community members. The root word for "embrace" is "-pet" and the ancestors are called "me" and "tot," meaning "mother" and "father." Significantly, the shaman is called "Hpetom" or "embracer" in curing ceremonies and the patient calls him "tot." Parents are called "me" and "tot" in family rituals and godparents are called "me" and "tot" in baptismal and wedding ceremonies.[13] In Zinacantan "totilmeiletik" is a word applied to both the ancestral gods and the ritual advisers of the cargo-holders.[14] A ritual adviser is called 'totilmeil" in Chamula as well.[15]

The use of "mayoletik" or "assistants" is a third way in which varied types of ceremonies reflect the concept of the ancestral gods' caring for the *naguals*. The ancestral gods have "mayoletik," hummingbirds and night-flying moles, who feed and water the animal spirits and summon the inner soul of potential shamans to take the oath of office. The president, head of the civil-religious hierarchy, parallels the ancestral gods as is indicated by his title "totik preserente." When he handles disputes in front of the "cabildo," he has twelve "mayoletik" to run errands for him and arrest culprits. During a curing ceremony, the shaman is called "totik" or "meik" and his assistants, relatives of the patient, are called "mayoletik."[16] Perhaps elders, healers and leaders of the civil-religious hierarchy are also conceived of as "mayoletik," since they are believed to have hummingbirds as *naguals* and they aid the ancestral gods in caring for the community and punishing wrongdoers.

Belief in good *naguals* who punish for the sake of justice is widespread. Guiteras-Holmes indicates the existence of this belief in San Pedro Chenalhó, when she says that "totilmeil" is applied to the ancestral god, as well as to every man whose soul is the hummingbird, the caretaker of all *naguals*.[17] Pedranos believe that by holding office one acquires "heat" along with power and prestige, and with this "heat" comes the responsibility of shielding people from evil.[18] Thus, when Manuel was president of San Pedro, he called the elders and told them to pray for the sins of the people.[19] A belief in good *naguals* has also been reported in Chamula, where "petomes" and "kuchomes," being the smartest and most competent animals, take care of the others; all curers have these types of animal-spirit-companions.[20] In Larrainzar, too, the animal-spirit-companions of important people care for those of lesser people.[21] This ability to protect also implies the ability to punish. For instance, it has been reported that in Oxchuc, elders and chiefs can know the thoughts and actions of their subordinates and mete out punishment for misbehavior by causing illness or other misfortune.[22]

The ancestral gods of their assistants, the hummingbird *naguals* of influential people, punish men for specific types of misbehavior. The major sins are: quarreling with kinsmen; failing to bathe and put on clean clothes regularly; mishandling maize; failing to take ritual duties seriously;[23] stealing, having illicit sexual relations; and trying to elevate oneself over the rest particularly in the ownership of material goods.[24] Thus, disease often indicates wrongdoing on the part of the sick person. The curing of illnesses provides a major means of social control since "wrongdoing" must be eliminated in order to procure relief.

The curing shaman is believed to be the only person who can communicate directly with the ancestral gods. Intimately informed about the patient's affairs he has complete control over the diagnosis, cause and cure of the illness.[25] The patient, by confessing his sins and praying to the ancestral gods for pardon, achieves psychological relief. Also, the ritual patterns require the cooperation and good will of the patient's kinsmen with whom he has, in many cases, been quarreling.[26] Thus, the shaman actually mediates disputes within families and kin-groups so that many litigations are resolved out of court.

Curing ceremonies also eliminate envy of wealthy men by stripping them of their surplus. For instance, if a rich man has refused to share his wealth, other members of his community will start gossiping about his moral decadence intimating that he must have acquired his wealth by devious means, or even that he has connections with the devil. This gossip can readily lead the man to become psychosomatically ill from too much aggravation. The curer will prescribe a costly ceremony as a means of appeasing the ancestral gods whom his patient has obviously angered. Besides curing the patient, the ceremonies eliminate the cause of his illness, i.e., his surplus wealth; restore his good relations with others by bringing everyone together to share rum and food; and restore his reputation as a "good man."

The belief in evil *naguals* as another cause of illness is also widespread. Vogt reports the Zinacanteco belief in "pukuhetik," or evil spirits: the "poslom," which is a ball of fire that travels at night and hits people causing a bad swelling; and "blackmen," who soar out of caves at dusk in search of food and companions.[27] Holland reports these same spirits for Larrainzar, adding that they are the *naguals* of evil, powerful people. Manuel, one of the more progressive thinkers of San Pedro Chenalhó, is rebelling against "those ideas about the ti'bal and that they eat people" because "the people live in dread and apprehension" as a result of them.[28] Even Manuel does not actually disbelieve in the evil forces; he merely thinks that their effects can be counteracted by good behavior and prayer. Manuel equates "Pukuh" and "Poslob" with a death-causing, evil sorcerer whose strength is equal to God's.[29] In Chamula, bad or aggressive men and especially those who quarrel often, are believed to have a "pukuj" for a *nagual*, while witches have "kibales" and "selomes" for *naguals*.[30] Kibales can change into "poslomes" or balls of fire. "Poslomes" are the highest, strongest *naguals* and eclipses are explained by the "poslomes" fighting the sun and moon and causing people to die.[31]

The fear of being considered a witch, i.e., a person who uses his *nagual* to harm others, forces people to maintain respectful and proper behavior with everyone and in all situations.

As has been shown, the belief and practice of witchcraft pervades all Tzeltal and Tzotzil communities. Since a man does not necessarily reveal his *nagual* to others,[32] any person may be suspected of witchcraft.[33] A powerful person must then be particularly careful always to act in a conventional manner. Since leaders and curers are known to have powerful *naguals*, they are more likely to be suspected of witchcraft. Curers have been known to murder a fellow curer as a witch and receive public approval of their action simply because the victim had altered a ritual. Any man who becomes sick or suffers some misfortune may attribute his ill-luck to witchcraft and start rumors about the person whom he holds responsible.

The socially accepted form of witch killing is ambush by a group of men after they have been drinking with the victim. Immediately after the killing, the community leaders judge the testimony by the family and neighbors of the victim and killers to assess their respective characters. If the killers have maintained good social relations while the victim has not, the community leaders will sanction the murder for the purpose of ridding the community of a witch.[34] Thus, the fear of either being harmed by a witch or being accused of witchcraft keeps everyone alert to the necessity of conventional behavior at all times.

To summarize, it is clear that concepts relating to the *nagual* or animal-spirit-companion are instrumental in maintaining harmonious social relations in the Tzeltal and Tzotzil communities of Chiapas, Mexico. The family, patrilineal group, waterhole group, and community group have counterparts in the supernatural society of *naguals* and ancestral gods.

Each social unit has periodic ceremonies for the purpose of

praying to the ancestral gods and these ceremonies give the members a sense of belonging. Participants in baptismal, wedding, and curing ceremonies have roles symbolizing the relationships between the ancestral gods and the *naguals*.

The ritual advisers who assist the cargoholders are compared to the hummingbirds who assist the ancestral gods. When they settle disputes, the presidente and the curing shaman are both likened to the ancestral gods.

Since disease is believed to result from an injury to a person's *nagual* and since the *nagual* is generally injured because a person has been quarreling with kinsmen, has been disloyal to his spouse, or has been trying to elevate himself above others, curing a disease involves restoring social harmony.

Since anyone may be a witch, each person is careful to avoid quarrels or situations which may lead to personal grudges against them to protect their *naguals*. At the same time, everyone must behave properly at all times and keep on good terms with his family and neighbors so that he will not be accused of being a witch.

The large number of murders sanctioned by the community leaders on the grounds that the victim is a witch is perhaps the most dramatic evidence of the *nagual* concept as a means of social control.

BIBLIOGRAPHY

1. Cancian, Frank. *Economics and Prestige in a Maya Community.* 1965. Stanford University Press. Stanford, Calif.
2. Foster, George. Nagualism in Mexico and Guatemala. 1944. *Acta Americana*: 2: 85–103.
3. Guiteras-Holmes, Calixta. "Organización Social de Tzeltales y Tzotziles," América Indigena, Vol. VIII, enero 1948, Núm. 1, Mexico, D.r.
4. Guiteras-Holmes, Calixta. *Perils of the Soul: The World View of a Tzotzil Indian.* Chicago, 1961.
5. Holland, W. "Tonalismo y Nagualismo entre los Indios Tzotziles de Larrainzer, Chiapas, Mexico." *Estudios de Cultura Maya 1*: 167–181.
6. Nash, Manning. "Witchcraft as Social Process in a Tzeltal Community." América Indígena 20: 121–126. 1960.
7. Pozas, Ricardo. *Chamula, un Pueble Indio de los Altos de Chiapas.*

8. Redfield, R. & Villa Rojas. "Notes on the Ethnography of Tzeltal Communities of Chiapas." 1943.
9. Villa Rojas. "Kinship and Nagualism in a Tzeltal Community." 1947.
10. Vogt, Evon Z. *Zinacantan: A Maya Community in the Highlands of Chiapas.* 1969. The Belknap Press of Harvard University Press. Cambridge, Mass.

FOOTNOTES

1. Pozas, 1962: 191.
2. Guiteras-Holmes, 1961: 299.
3. Guiteras-Holmes, 1961: 300.
4. Guiteras-Holmes, 1961: 288.
5. Vogt, 1969: 371.
6. Vogt, 1962: 372.
7. Vogt, 1969: 493.
8. Vogt, 1969: 593.
9. Holland, 1961: 169.
10. Vogt, 1969: 390.
11. Vogt, 1969: 141.
12. Vogt, 1969: 144.
13. Vogt, 1969: 577.
14. Vogt, 1969: 579.
15. Pozas, 1962: 165.
16. Vogt, 1969: 579.
17. Guiteras-Holmes, 1961: 292.
18. Guiteras-Holmes, 1961: 73.
19. Guiteras-Holmes, 1961: 255.
20. Pozas, 1962: 193.
21. Holland, 1963: 113.
22. Villa Rojas, 1947: 584.
23. Vogt, 1969: 301.
24. Villa Rojas, 1947: 585.
25. Vogt, 1969: 474.
26. Vogt, 1969: 273.
27. Vogt, 1969: 304.
28. Guiteras-Holmes, 1961: 256.
29. Guiteras-Holmes, 1961: 293.
30. Pozas, 1962: 191.
31. Pozas, 1962: 192.
32. Nash, 1960: 121.
33. Holland, 1961: 171.
34. Nash, 1960: 121.

FOREWORD TO
"MEDICINE THROUGHOUT ANTIQUITY"
by
DR. MAX NEUBURGER

The author of this volume is one of the few practitioners who combines a lively interest in the history of medicine with sound and solid method in historical research. For quite some time now, he has been proving his capacity along these lines. Each of his technical articles in the Archives of Ophthalmology shows historical background in keeping with the standard set by Hirschberg. The author's publications dealing with medicine among the Hebrews rest on deep and critical scholarship, reminiscent of Preuss. Gordon's book Romance of Medicine combines enjoyable readability with richness of content. It has been widely acclaimed, gone through two editions, and is being translated into Spanish. Its virtues characterize, but to a still greater extent, this distinguished and comprehensive work: Medicine throughout Antiquity.

This book, in many ways, is distinctive in the literature on medical history. Hitherto, writers have provided only the briefest account of prehistoric medicine and, after a more or less sketchy description of medicine in the Orient, give us the main chapters of ancient medicine: those on Greece and Rome. In Gordon's work, however, pre-Greek medicine fills Part I, comprising 429 pages. In Part II, he admirably describes Greek, Alexandrian, and Roman medicine from the sources and with reference to general cultural environment; to this he adds an account of Talmudic medicine.

Gordon distinguishes three periods in ancient medicine: (1) the prehistoric, starting from the earliest times; (2) the protohistoric; and (3) the age that began with Ionic philosophy and ended with the fall of Rome. He has worked through a vast body of material, with reference to the results of the latest research on the subject.

His work is critical, and in some ways organized and synthesized along completely new lines. Time and again, Gordon throws light on modern medicine, and at every turn the reader feels that the book hails from the pen of a practicing physician.

Benjamin Lee Gordon, M.D.: Medicine throughout Antiquity, Philadelphia, 1949.

CHAPTER 7

Dr. Solomon Drowne's Journal on the Privateer Hope

by

MAURICE BEAR GORDON, A.B., M.D.*

THE SEARCH FOR THE *JOURNAL*

Some months after Admiral E. M. Eller requested that I write an article reconstructing "Naval and Maritime Medicine during the Revolution" for inclusion in Naval Documents of the American Revolution, I vaguely remembered of having read many years previously of a naval journal which had been kept by an American surgeon of the Revolution, Doctor Solomon Drowne, which had been mentioned by his descendant, Brigadier General H. Russell Drowne, and listed as in the possession of the General. I knew that the time of the General's publication roughly coincided with the 1949 publication of the first printing of my "Aesculapius Comes to the Colonies: The Story of the Early Days of Medicine in the Thirteen Original Colonies." A painstaking investigation revealed that an article entitled "Doctor Solomon Drowne: A Surgeon of the Revolution" was indeed published by Brigadier General H. Russell Drowne in the January 1949 issue of *The Bulletin of The Fort Ticonderoga Museum.*[1] On page 111 of *The Bulletin*, Gen-

---

*Maurice Bear Gordon, M.D. practices Internal Medicine in Ventnor, N. J. He is the author of "Aesculapius Comes to the Colonies: The Early Days of Medicine in the Thirteen Original Colonies."

eral Drowne, the great, great grandson of the Revolutionary Doctor, stated that he had in his possession the original *Journal* of his ancestor who in the fall of 1780 went on a cruise as surgeon on the privateer *Hope.*

On June 13, 1969 I wrote to the Pentagon inquiring as to the address of Brigadier General H. Russell Drowne. After numerous communications with the Department of the Army, first with the Pentagon and later with the Office of the Adjutant General, U.S. Army Administration Center, St. Louis, Missouri, I received a letter dated October 22, 1969 stating that Brigadier General H. Russell Drowne had died on April 7, 1968. This letter listed the address of his widow in New York City. On October 28, 1969 I wrote to General Drowne's widow and she promptly replied on November 1, 1969 that, whereas she was not aware of the location of the *Journal,* the General's younger son lived in Short Hills, New Jersey and that he had various family documents and perhaps might be able to help me with my search. On November 5, 1969 I wrote to this son and he answered by stating that he was not certain as to where the *Journal* was located but that I should try the Library at Brown University since it is the repository of a large Drowne Family collection.

On November 14, 1969 I wrote to the Brown University Library and received a cordial letter dated November 21, 1969 from Mrs. Christine D. Hathaway, Special Collections Librarian, that Brown University Library indeed did have the original *Journal* in its possession and that she would furnish me with photographs of same.

It is of more than coincidental interest to note that Mrs. Hathaway proved to be a Drowne descendant herself and I was able to give her the address of the Drowne descendant in Short Hills, New Jersey, to permit renewal of old family ties!

So ended the search for the *Journal* of Doctor Solomon Drowne on the privateer *Hope.*

BIOGRAPHICAL DATA

Dr. Solomon Drowne (1753–1834), Rhode Island's most illustrious surgeon of the Revolution, was born in Providence on March 11, 1753. In 1773, at the age of 20, he graduated from

Rhode Island College (now Brown University) and he later received his M.D. degree from the University of Pennsylvania. He served during the Revolution as surgeon under Dr. John Morgan, Director-General of New York Hospitals at the time of evacuation by the Americans. In July 1776, he performed the first operation at The New York Hospital—an arm amputation. He then served as surgeon in the Rhode Island Hospital and in Sullivan's Expedition on Rhode Island and in the regiments of Colonel Crary and Colonel Atwell.

It was during Sullivan's Expedition that Dr. Drowne performed daring and successful brain surgery. A soldier who had received a severe skull injury was trephined by Dr. Drowne. As the surgeon removed the depressed bone fragment from his patient's brain thus relieving the intracranial pressure, the injured soldier, prior to regaining consciousness, finished shouting a command which had been interrupted by the battlefield injury. Dr. Drowne then hammered in a Spanish silver coin to protect the brain from the missing skull fragment. The patient not only survived the operation but lived over thirty years afterwards.

In the Fall of 1780, at the age of 27, Dr. Drowne became part of the story of naval medicine during the Revolution by serving on the privateer sloop *Hope* and he left a journal of this voyage.

"Journal of a Cruise in the Fall of 1780" is a short but utterly charming piece of literature written by a landlubber physician at sea for the first time. The voyage of the sloop *Hope* started in Providence on Tuesday, October 3, 1780 and terminated in the same city on Monday, October 22, 1780, just nineteen terror-stricken days later. The voyage was successful because a British snow[2] was captured as a prize. The snow had sailed from Kingston, Jamaica some forty odd days prior to its capture as a part of a fleet bound for New York. Captain William Small and nine crew were captured as were "four excellent four pounders." The cargo of the snow was primarily liquid and consisted of "149 Puncheons, 23 Hogsheads, 3 Quarter Casks and 9 barrels of Rum and 20 Hogsheads Muscovado Sugar."

The medical references in the *Journal* are two in number:

On October 4, 1780, Surgeon Drowne notes "——— a heavy sea from the southward. I begin to be excessively sea-sick, but do not take my station upon the lee quarter till that side is pretty well manned. This is a sickness, that is indeed enough to depress the spirits even of the brave." On October 5, 1780, he states: "Fresh Breezes and cloudy. Treble reefed Mainsail. Excessive sickness, Hove too. A heavy sea with squalls of rain."

On October 20, 1780, Surgeon Drowne records: "About sunset I go on board the Snow, at Captain Small's request to do something for his Rheumatic knee, and see a very sick boy: after prescribing for him, examining the medicine box, giving directions, etc. return to the Sloop."

That Dr. Drowne did not really approve of the morality of privateering is evidenced from an entry in the *Journal* dated October 11, 1780: "If Virtue is the doing good to others, privateering cannot be justified upon the principles of Virtue;—though I know it is not repugnant to the *Laws of Nations*, but rather deemed policy amongst warring powers thus to distress each other, regardless of the suffering individual. But however agreeable to, and supportable by the rights of war; yet, when individuals come thus to despoil individuals of their property, 'tis hard:—the cruelty then appears, however, political."

In 1783 Dr. Drowne was elected to the Board of Fellows of Brown University. In 1784 he visited British hospitals and medical schools and attended lectures given by the English medical scholars. In May 1785 he visited Belgium and Holland for a like purpose and then he went to France where he often visited Benjamin Franklin at whose abode he met Thomas Jefferson.

He then returned to practice in Providence until 1788 when he moved to Marietta, Ohio, for almost a year. Following this he returned to Providence where he practiced until 1792 at which time he retired and moved to Morgantown, West Virginia. In 1801 he settled in Foster, Rhode Island. In 1811 he became Professor of Materia Medica and Botany at Brown University and in 1819, at the age of 66, he was elected to the convention which established the National Pharmacopoeia by the Rhode Island Medical Society of which organization he was vice president.

Dr. Solomon Drowne died in Foster, Rhode Island on February 5, 1834 one month short of the age of 81.

THE JOURNAL

In 1872, ninety-two years after the writing of the *Journal*, a grandson of Dr. Solomon Drowne, Henry Thayer Drowne, published a good transcription of the *Journal* on the private press of Charles L. Moreau, New York. Because of a number of minor errors and some obviously intentional corrections of the original manuscript, this transcription is not employed in the present article.

JOURNAL OF A CRUISE IN THE FALL OF 1780

Tuesday, Octr. 3^d. Sailed from Providence on board the Sloop *Hope*, mounting seven guns. Wind at N.E. drizzly, dirty weather. Outsailed Mr. John Brown in his famous boat. Put about for Captain Munro, and take Mr. Brown & Captain S. Smith on board, who dine with us. Some time after noon Captain Munro comes on board, and a few glasses of good wishes founded on Hope having circled, Colonel Nightingale, etc. depart, and we proceed on our course. Towards evening come to anchor between Dutch-Island and Conanicut, to get in readiness for the Sea. Officiate as Clerk copying the Articles, etc.

4th. This morning sail from Dutch-Island harbour; at 7 pass the Light-house walls on Beaver Tail; Wind N.E. hazy Weather,—a heavy sea from the southward. I begin to be excessively sea-sick, but do not take my station upon the lee quarter till that side is pretty well manned. This is a sickness, that is indeed enough to depress the spirits even of the brave.

5th. Fresh Breezes and cloudy. Treble reefed Mainsail. Excessive sickness. Hove too. A heavy sea with squalls of rain.

6th. Keep the Cabbin. Strong Gales and squally; still lying by. Saw a Ship & made sail from her; then brought too again.

Journal of a Cruize in ye Fall of 1780.

Tuesday Octr 3. Sailed from Providence on board ye Sloop Hope, mounting seven guns. Wind at N.E. drizzly, dirty weather. Outsailed Mr John Brown in his famous boat. Put about for Capt. Munro, and take Mr Brown & Capt. Smith on board, who dine with us. Some time afternoon Capt. Munro comes on board, and a few glasses of good wishes founded on Hope having circled, — Col. Nightingale &c. depart, and we proceed on our course. Towards evening come to anchor between Dutch Island and Conanicut, to get in readiness for ye Sea. officiate as Clk copying ye Articles, &c.

4th This morning sail from Dutch Island harbour, at 7 pass ye Light-house walls, on Beaver Tail; Wind N.E. hazy Weather, & heavy sea, from ye southwd I begin to be excessively seasick, but do not take my station upon ye lee quarter till that side is pretty well manned. This is a sickness, that is indeed enough to depress the spirits even of ye brave.

5th Fresh Breezes & cloudy. Unable to do anything. Excessive sickness. Hove too. A heavy sea with squalls of rain.

6th Keep ye Cabbin. Strong Gales & squally, still lying by. Saw a Ship & made sail from her, then brought too again.

7th. Get the Topmast down; balance the Mainsail and lie too:—put our guns in the hold, etc. Afternoon.—The Gale becomes violent. Only one long practiced seaman on board, who says he ever knew it more tempestuous. Nail down our hatches and secure everything in the best manner possible. Have a hole cut through the store room to open a communication fore and aft below deck. The Storm increases. Ship a Sea which carries away some of our crane irons. Get our Axes into the Cabbin, ready to cut away the Mast should there be occasion. A becoming fortitude in general predominates on board, though horror stalks around.—They who go down to the sea in ships, do indeed see the wonders of the LORD in the deep.—

The description of a Tempest translated by Boileau from Longinus, occurs to my mind with peculiar energy.

2/ 7:th. Get y.e Topmast down; ballance y.e
Mains.l and lye to: — put our guns in
the hold, &c. afternoon. —The Gale becomes
violent. Only one long practised seaman
on board, who says he ever knew it
more tempestuous. Nail down our
hatches and secure every thing in y.e best
manner possible. Have a hole cut thro'
the store room to open a communication
fore and aft. below deck. The Storm
increases. Ship a sea which carries
away some of our crane irons. Get our
axes into y.e Cabbin, ready to cut
away y.e Mast shou'd there be occasion.
A becoming fortitude in general
predominates on board, tho' horror
stalks around. ———. They who go
down to the sea in ships, do indeed
see the wonders of y.e Lord in y.e deep. —

The description of a tempest translated
by Boileau from Longinus, occurs
to my mind with peculiar
energy.   Comme

104

Commel'on voit les Flots, soûleves par l'Orage,
Fondre sur un Vaisseau qui s'oppose à leur Rage,
Le vent avec Fureur dans les Voiles fremit;
La Mer blanchit d'écume, et l'Air au loin gémit;
Le Matelot troublé, que son Art abandonne,
Croit voir dans chaque Flot la Mort qui l'environne.[3]
I like this description because there are no little, triffling incidents thrown in. 'Tis short and energetic—grand & forcive like the storm itself.————One, now, can scarce refrain from envying the Husbandman, who, folded on his bed of placid quiet, hears the wind whistle round his steady Mansion, whilst our ears are assailed by its rude howling through the Cordage[4]—; our vessel tossed upon the foaming Surges. Thrice happy rural life! and too happy countrymen, did they but know their happiness————The gale moderates; the wind shifts and the sea begins to be appeased. ————GOD of Nature! who that sees thy greatness on the wide extended Ocean, but must be filled with Adoration; and feel a submission of heart to thy eternal orders.
8th. Moderate Weather after the Storm.

Comme l'on voit les Flots, soûlevez par l'Orage,
Fondre sur un Vaisseau qui s'oppose à leur Rage,
Le vent avec Fureur dans les Voiles fremit;
La Mer blanchit d'écume, & l'Air au loin gémit;
Le Matelot troublé, que son Art abandonne,
Croit voir dans chaque Flot la Mort qui l'environne.

I like this description because there are
no little, trifling incidents thrown in.
'Tis short and energetic — grand & forcive
like the Storm itself. --- One now can
scarce refrain from envying y.ᵉ Husbandman,
who, folded on his bed of placid quiet, hears the
wind whistle round his steady Mansion, whilst
our ears are assailed by it's rude howling
thro' y.ᵉ Cordage — our vessel toss'd upon
the foaming Surges. Thrice happy rural
Life! and too happy countrymen, did
they but know their happiness ——
The gale moderates; the wind shifts,
and the sea begins to be appeased. — ·
GOD of Nature! who that sees thy
greatness on the wide extended Ocean,
but must be filled with Adoration;
and feel a submission of heart to
thy eternal orders. ———
8.ᵗʰ Moderate Weather after y.ᵉ Storm.
                              9 et

Get our clothes, etc. out to dry. Cloudy still.—Our Mariners wonder we came off so well as we did; and indeed, we escaped to admiration, owing in some measure to the goodness of our vessel, and the taking every precaution, previous to the severity of the gale. Towards evening a Sail seen from mast-head: set sail & stand for her.

9th. "Post Nubila, *Phoebus*."—A beautiful morning. How chearing are the beams of the Sun! I view him almost with the Sentiments of a Persian.—Those surly billows that erewhile buffetted us to and fro, and would suffer us no peace,—are composed as the infant that has bawled itself to rest.————A large number of Whale of the Spermaceeti kind playing round us this morning:—and let them sport;—the Father of the Universe has given them the expanded Ocean for the wide Scene of their happiness.————Nothing of said Sail to be seen.—Have an Observation for the first time. Latitude 38°. 57′. 37′. My Variation Chart of no use for want

4[/] Get our cloaths, &c. out to dry. Cloudy still.—Our Mariners wonder we came off so well as we did; and indeed, we escaped to admiration, owing in some measure to ye goodness of our vessel; and ye taking every precaution, previous to ye severity of the gale.   Towards evening a Sail seen from mast-head: set sail & stand for her.

9th "Post Nubila, Phœbus."—A beautiful morning. How chearing are ye beams of the Sun! I view him almost with the Sentiments of a Bramin. [Persian]—Those surly billows that erewhile buffetted us to and fro, and wou'd suffer us no peace,—are composed as the infant that has brawled itself to rest. - - - A large number of Whale of ye Spermaceti kind playing round us this morning:—And let them sport;—the Father of ye Universe has given them the expanded Ocean for the wide Scene of their happiness.—Nothing of ye Sail to be seen. Have an Observation for the first time. Lat^o 38.57.

My Variation Chart of no use for want of

of an Azimuth Compass. Afternoon, discover a Ship standing to the eastward.

10th. No remarkable occurrence. Lat.—54'.

11th. Whilst at Dinner, a Sail cried. Immediately give chace, and discover another. One, a sloop which bears down upon us; the other a brigg. Make every preparation for an engagement; but, on approaching & hailing the Sloop, she proved to be the Randolph, Captain Fosdick from N(ew) London,—mounting 18 four pounders [140 tons.]. The Brig, with only two guns, her prize from England, taken at 8 o'clock this morning. Captain Fosdick says her Cargo amounted to £20,000 Sterling. What good & ill fortune were consequent on that capture!—Hard for those poor fellows, their tedious Voyage being just accomplished, thus to have their brightening prospect clouded in a moment. If Virtue is the doing good to others, privateering cannot be justified upon the principles of Virtue;—though I know it is not repugnant to the *Laws of Nations*, but rather deemed policy amongst

of an Azimuth Compass. Afternoon 5. I
discover a Ship standing to ye eastward.
10th. No remarkable Occurrence. Lat. — 54. 9 ght:
11th Whilst at Dinner, a Sail cried. Im-
:mediately give chace, and discover
another. One, a Sloop which bears down
upon us; the other a brigg. Make
every preperation for an engagement;
but, on approaching & hailing ye Sloop,
she proved to be the Randolph, Cap^tn
Fosdick from N. London — mounting 18
[140 tons.]
four pounders. The Brig, with only two
guns, her prize from England, taken at
8 oʼclick this morning. Capt. Fosdick
says her Cargo amounted to £ 20,000 Sterlg.
What good & ill fortune were consequent
on that capture! — Hard for those poor
fellows, their tedious Voyage being just
accomplished, thus to have their brightening prospect clouded in a moment.
If Virtue is the doing good to others,
privateering cannot be justified upon
the principles of Virtue; — tho' I know it
is not repugnant to the Laws of Nations,
but rather deemed policy amongst

remarkable

warring powers thus to distress each other, regardless of the suffering individual. But however agreeable to, and supportable by the rights of war; yet, when individuals come thus to despoil individuals of their property, 'tis hard:—the cruelty then appears, however, political.

12th. Early this morning two sail in sight, a Ship & Brig. Chace them chief of the day to no purpose. We conclude they sail well, and may be bound to Philadelphia. Lat. 39. 6. Soundings 19 fathoms. Lost sight of the Randolph by the chace.

13th. A foggy morning & Scotch mist.[5] Clears away pleasant. Lat. 39. 31. This Afternoon a Sloop discovered under the lee bow standing before the wind: All hands upon deck preparing for the chace:—but little wind so the oars are to be plyed. I must go and see how we come on.—Night obliges us to give over the pursuit.

14th. A sail seen from Mast-head; proves a Ship. We chase. Catch a Herring-Hog,[6] which makes us a fine Breakfast, and

warring powers thus to distress
each other, regardless of the suffering individual. But however
agreeable to, and supportable by
the rights of war; yet, when individuals come thus to despoil individuals of their property, 'tis hard:—the
cruelty then appears however political.
12th . Early this morning two sail in
sight, a Ship & Brig. Chace them chief
of the day to no purpose. We conclude
they sail well, and may be bound to
Philadelphia. Lat. 39.6 Sounding, 19 fm
Lost sight of ye Randolph by ye Chace.
13th A foggy morning & Scotch mist.
Clears away pleasant. Lat. 39.31. This Aftern—
a Sloop discovered under ye lee bow standing before ye wind: all hands upon deck
preparing for the chace,—but little wind
so the oars are to be plyed. I must go
and see how we come on. —— Night
obliges us to give over the pursuit,—
——— A sail seen from Mast-head; proves
a Ship. We chace. Catch a Herring-Hog,
which makes us a fine Breakfast, and
dinner

dinner for the whole crew. Another sail heaves in sight. Upon a nearer approach the Ship appears to be of the line. Several in sight: Towards evening signal guns heard. We take them to be men of War, standing in, NW by W. Longitude by reckoning 73°. 30″. Latitude 39. 34″. 26 fathoms. A pleasant moon-light Evening. Spend it in walking the Quarter Deck.

15th. A pleasant day. See a Sail to windward, as she rather approaches us we lie a hull for her. I think it is more agreeable waiting for them, than rowing after them. Get a fishing line under way: catch a Hake[7] and a few dog-fish.[8] It being Sunday, try the efficacy of a clean shirt, in order to be something like folks ashore. Give chase, as the vessel comes down rather slow. On approaching discover her to be a Snow. She hauls her wind and stands from us; —sails very heavy, and Captain Munro is sanguine in the belief we shall make a prize of her. Get everything in readiness to board her. There seems something awful in the preparation for an attack, and the immediate prospect of action. She hauls up her courses and hoists English Colours. I take my station in the Cabin; where,

dinner for y.e whole crew. Another sail heav.d
in sight. Upon a nearer approach the
Ship appears to be of y.e Line. Several in sight:
Towards evening signal guns heard. We take
them to be men of War, standing in, NWbW. —
Longitude by reconing 73° 30' Lat.° 39..34.26f.m
A pleasant moon-light Evening. Spend
it in walking y.e 2.d Deck.

15.th A pleasant day. See a sail to windwd
as she rather approaches us we lie
a hull for her. I think it is more
agreeable waiting for them, than rowing
after them. Get a fishing line under
way: catch a Hake and a few dogfish.
It being Sunday, try y.e efficacy of a
clean shirt in order to be something
like folks ashore. Give chace, as the
vessel comes down rather slow. On
approaching discover her to be a Snow.
She hauls her wind and stands from us; sails very
heavy, and Cap.t Homo is sanguine in y.e belief
we shall make a prize of her. Get everything
in readiness to board her. There seems something
awful in the preparation for an attack, and
the immediate prospect of action. She hauls
up her courses and hoists English Colours.
I take my station in the Cabin; where,
                          remain

114

remain not long before I hear the Huzza on deck in consequence of her striking. Send our boat for the Captain & his papers. She sailed from Kingston, Jamaica, upwards of 40 days since, in a fleet, and was bound to N(ew) York: Captain William Small, commander. She has ten men on board & four excellent four pounders. Her Cargo consists of 149 Puncheons,[9] 23 Hogsheads,[10] 3 Quarter Casks and 9 barrels of Rum, and 20 Hogsheads Muscovado Sugar.[11] Send two prize Masters and ten men on board, get the prisoners on board our Vessel, and taking the prize in tow, stand towards Egg Harbour. We hardly know what to do with the prize: the wind shifting a little we stand to the eastward.

16th. Keep an eastern course, to try to get her into our harbour if possible. Now we are terribly apprehensive of seeing a sail.— About sunset a sail seen from mast-head, which excites no small anxiety. Cast off the Snow's hawser, etc.—however night coming on and seeing no more of said sail, pursue our course. Sound, 42 fathoms of water.

17th. Strong Gales at N.N.W. & very cold. Latitude 40°. 30″. Afternoon moderates somewhat:—take the old Snow in tow again. We expect to bring up somewhere in the neighbourhood of Martha's Vineyard.—A squall with hail & snow comes up which splits the Snow's jibb to pieces. A little bird came on board rendered quite tame by it's long hazzardous flight. Amuse myself with looking over a

& remain not long before I hear ye. Huzza
on deck in consequence of her striking. ~~the~~
Send our boat for the Capt.n & his papers. She
sailed from Kingston, Jamaica, upwards of 40
days since, in a fleet, and was bound to N. York:
Capt. Wm. Smail, commander. She has ten men
on b.d and & hour excellent four pounders. Her
cargo consists of 149 Puncheons, 23 Hhds 3 2 Tierces
and 4 bls of Rum, and 20 Hhds Muscovado Sugar.
Send ~~two~~ prize masters and ten men on board,
get the prisoners on board our Vessel, and
taking ye prize in tow, stand towards Egg
Harbour. We hardly know what to do with
the prize: the wind shifting a little we
stand to ye eastward.
16th Theref an eastern course, to try to get
her into our harbour if possible. Now
we are terribly apprehensive of seeing a
sail. — About sunset a sail seen from
mast-head, which excites no small anxiety.
Cast off the Snow's hawser, &c. — however night
coming on and seeing no more of sd. sail, pur-
=sue our course. Sound, 42 fathm = of water.
17th Strong Gales at N.N.W. & very cold. Lat.d
40°..30" Afternoon moderates somewhat:
take ye old Snow in tow again. We expect
to bring up somewhere in ye neighbourhood
of Martha's Vineyard. — A squall with
hail & snow comes up which splits ye Snow's
jibb to pieces. A little bird came on board
rendered quite tame by it's long, hazzardous
flight. Amuse myself with looking over
                                                    a

Quarter Waggoner, taken out of the snow. Take a drink of Grogg, made of snow-water.[12] Very heavy squalls indeed this night, with a rough, bad sea; obliged to cast off the dull Snow and let her go her own pace. about 42 fathoms water. Sleep little.

18th. Boisterous weather still, a tumbling sea going. Feel qualmish. Latitude 40. 40.—The wind so contrary that we make but slow advances towards our desired haven. Just as I was pleasing myself with the idea of a speedy conclusion to this disagreeable cruise, a sail is cried, which perhaps will protract it, if not show us York in our way home. The sail appears to be a brig, and not standing for us, as we at first apprehended. We chase 'till night prevents. Lose sight of the Snow: fire signal guns, show false fires & a lantern, but see no answer.

19th. The Snow in sight this morning; run along side and take her in tow again. They say they answered our signals, 'though unseen by us. A pretty bird caught on board: the Carolina red bird. More moderate weather. Latitude 40. 30″. At this rate the West Indies will bring us up sooner than Martha's Vineyard or Nantucket. 46 fathoms. Have our Pistols hung up in the Cabbin, to be in readiness for the prisoners, should they take it into their heads to rise upon the watch in the night—

Dr Waggoner, taken out of ye snow. Take a drink
of Grogg made of snow water. Very heavy squalls
indeed this night, with a rough, bad Sea;
obliged to cast off the dull Snow and let
her go her own pace. About 42 fm water. keep little
18th. Boisterous weather still, a tumbling sea
going. Feel qualmish. Lat. 40.40. The wind
so contrary that we make but slow advances,
towards our desired haven. Just as I was
pleasing myself with the idea of a speedy
conclusion to this disagreeable cruise, a
sail is cried, which perhaps will protract
it, if not show us York in our way home.
The sail appears to be a brig, and not standing
for us, as we at first apprehended. We
chace 'till night prevents. Lose sight of
the Snow: fire signal guns, show false
fires & a lantern, but see no answer.
19th The Snow in sight this morning;
run along side and take her in tow
again. They say they answered our signals, though unseen by us. A pretty
bird caught on board: the Carolina redbird.
More moderate weather. Lat. 40.30. At this
rate ye West Indies will bring us up sooner
than Martha's Vineyard or Nantucket. 46 fm
Have our Pistols hung up in ye Cabin, to
be in readiness for the prisoners, should
they take it into their heads to rise upon
ye watch in the night ——————— 20th

20th. Thick weather, and the wind contrary. Depth of water, 17 fathoms. Surely we must be nigh some land; and were it not such weather, perhaps might see it. Latitude 39°. 59″. A good southwardly breeze last evening shoved us up to this latitude.—Here we are, becalmed and fairly lost: for whether we are to the eastward of Nantucket, or between Marthas Vineyard & Block Island, or the last & Montige point (a little to the southward of them all) is a matter in question amongst our Seamen. About sunset I go on board the Snow, at Captain Small's request to do something for his Rheumatic knee, and see a very sick boy; after prescribing for him, examining the medicine box, giving directions, etc. return to the Sloop.

21st. Very calm. Not a breath to ruffle the Ocean. How uneasy every one on board is, fearing to lose the prize; but, if we can't stir hence; others can't come here to molest us. 14 fathoms of water, with yellowish, small gravel stones, according to some the sign of Noman's land, to others of Montock.—I hope we shall know where we are, soon. The Horizon too hazy yet to see far.— Half past 10. At length the agreeable prospect presents itself. Martha's Vineyard, etc. full in view. What an excellent landfall! To one who was never out of sight of land a whole day before,— the seeing it again is very pleasing, though after only seventeen days deprivation. It is very disagreeable

10/ 20th Thick weather, and ye wind contrary.
Depth of water, 17 fathm Surely we must be nigh
some land; and were it not such weather,
perhaps might see it. Lat. 39°.59". A good south=
=wardly breeze last evening shoved us up to
this Latitude. — Here we are, becalmed and
fairly lost: for whether we are to ye eastward
of Nantucket or between Martha's Vineyard &
Block Island or ye East & Montage point (a lit:
tle to ye Sward of them all) is a matter in
question amongst our Seamen.   About
sunset I go on board ye Snow, at Capt. Small's
request to do something for his Rheumatic
knee, and see a very sick boy: after prescrib-
=ing for him, examining ye Medicine box,
giving directions, &c. return to ye Sloop.
21st Very calm. Not a breath to ruffle
the Ocean. How uneasy every one on
board is, fearing to lose ye prize: but, if
we can't stir hence; others can't come
here to molest us. 14 fathm water, with
yellowish, small gravel stones, according to
some ye sign of Noman's land, to others, of
Montock. I hope we shall know where
we are, soon. The Horizon too hazy yet to
see far.   — In part 10.. At length ye agreeable
prospect presents itself. Martha's Vineyard,
&c. full in view. What an excellent landfall!
To one who was never out of sight of land a
whole day before, — the seeing it again is
very pleasing, tho' after only seventeen
days deprivation. It is very disagreeable

tossing about in so small a Vessel at this season of the year. Latitude 41°. 17′. A pilot comes on board,—and soon after another; but too late. We go in between Nomans land and Gay-Head, so called from it's exhibiting variety of colours when the sun shines bright upon it, especially just after a rain.—Elizabeth Islands in sight on the Starboard side. Cuddy hunk the west most. 10 o'clock P.M. We now have Seconet point astern, therefore are safe: pass up the East side of Rhode Island. Our men are in uncommon spirits.—Anchor about a league up the passage.

22nd. Sunday. Very foggy. What wind there is, ahead. Weigh Anchor, and out oars.—A fair gentle breeze springs from the South. Pass through Bristol Ferry way with hard tugging about the middle of the afternoon: come to Anchor in the Bay, but where rendered uncertain by the fog having come up again.— About 6 o'clock Captain Munro & I, with four of the Hands set off for Providence in the boat: being envelloped in an uncommon thick fog, take a Compass & lantern on board;—but proceed not far, the smallness of the boat, and inexpertness of the rowers, occasioning a motion agitating our compass beyond use; therefore, are glad to find the way back to the Hope, which is effected by their fixing a lantern in the Shrouds, in consequence of our raising ours and hailing.

tossing about in so small a Vessel at this
season of y.e year. Lat.d 41°17'. A pilot comes
on board,— and soon after another; but too late.
We go in between Nomansland and Gay-Head,
so called from its exhibiting variety of colours
when y.e sun shines bright upon it, especially
just after a rain. Elizabeth Islands in sight
on y.e Starboard side. Cuddyhunk y.e westmost.
10 oClock P.M. We now have Seconet point
astern, therefor are safe: pass up y.e East
side of Rhoda Island. Our men are in un:
:common spirits.— Anchor about a league
up y.e passage.
22.d Sunday. Very foggy. What wind there is,
ahead. Weigh Anchor, and out oars.— A
fair gentle breeze springs up from y.e south.
pass through Bristol Ferry way with hard
tugging about y.e middle of y.e afternoon:
come to Anchor in y.e Bay, but where ren:
:dered uncertain by y.e fog having come up
again.— About 6 oClock Capt. Munro &
I, with four of y.e hands set off for Providence in
y.e boat: being invelloped in an uncommon
thick fog, take a Compass & lantern on board;
— but proceed not far, the smallness of y.e boat,
and inexpertness of y.e rowers, occasioning a
motion agitating our compass beyond use;
therefor, are glad to find y.e way back to y.e
Hope, which is effected by their fixing
a lantern in y.e shrouds, in consequence
of our raising ours and hailing. 23.?

23rd. Early, after breakfast, we set off again in the boat, with the compass, being still surrounded with an excessive thick fog. Run ashore to the Eastward of Nait's point, and mistake it for Conimicutt: however, arrive at Providence about 11 o'clock; it having cleared off very pleasant. Thus ends our short, but tedious cruise. At sunset the Sloop and Snow arrive, firing 13 cannon each.

12) 23.ᵈ Early, after breakfast, we set off
again in yᵉ boat, with yᵉ compass, being
still surrounded with an excessive
thick fog. Run ashore to yᵉ Eastward
of Nait's point, and mistake it for Conic-
=nientt: however, arrive at Providence
about 11 o'clock; it having cleared off very
pleasant. Thus ends our short, but tedi-
:ous cruise. At sunset the Sloop & Snow
arrive, firing 13 cannon each. ——

BIBLIOGRAPHY

1. Drowne, M. D., Solomon: Journal of a Cruise in the Fall of 1780 in the Private-Sloop of War, Hope, with "Notes" by Henry T. Drowne, Private Press of Charles L. Moreau, New York, 1872. In his notes to this volume, Henry T. Drowne refers to the following articles about Dr. Solomon Drowne: "by Dr. Parsons in the Providence Literary Journal, May 10, 1834; by Professor Goddard in his Writings and Biographical Notices; by the Rev. T. S. Drowne, D.D. in The Sketches of R. I. Physicians, in the N. Y. Letters during the American Revolution, and in Mr. Dawson's edition of Dring's Recollections of the Jersey Prison-Ship; by the Rev. C. C. Beaman in his Sketches of Foster, published in the Providence Journal; by the Rev. Edwin M. Stone in Vol. VI. of the Coll. R. I. Hist. Society; by the Hon. James W. Beekman in his Centenary Address before the N. Y. Hospital, 1871; also in the Biographical Dictionaries of the Rev. J. L. Blake, D.D., and of F. S. Drake; while honorable mention has been made of him in the Alumni Discourse of Judge Pitman in 1843, and the Centennial of President Sears in 1864; also in the Rev. Dr. F. Vinton's Oration before the Sons of Rhode Island, and in Mr. R. A. Guild's Life of Manning, and his History of Brown University."
2. Drowne, H. R.: Doctor Solomon Drowne, A Surgeon of the Revolution, *The Bulletin of the Fort Ticonderoga Museum*, Vol. VIII, No. 3, Jan. 1949, pp. 110–112.
3. Gordon, M. B.: Aesculapius Comes to the Colonies: The Early Days of Medicine in the Thirteen Original Colonies, Ventnor, 1949; New York, 1970; pp. 271–273.
4. Beekman, James William: Centenary Address presented to the Society of The New York Hospital on July 24, 1871.

FOOTNOTES

1. Vol. VIII, No. 3, pp. 110 to 112. This article is listed as having been abstracted from an article published in *The New York National Guardsman*.
2. A "snow" is a square-rigged vessel differing from a "brig" only by having a try-sail mast close abaft the mainmast.
3. A proper transcription and translation by my beloved brother, Professor Cyrus H. Gordon, is here appended:
   Comme l'on voit les Flots, soulevés par l'Orage,
   As one sees the waves raised by the storm,
   Fondre sur un Vaisseau qui s'oppose à leur Rage,
   dash on a ship which confronts their rage,

> *Le vent avec Fureur dans les Voiles frémit;*
> the wind shakes with fury in the sails;
> *La Mer blanchit d'écume, et l'Air au loin gémit;*
> the sea is white with foam, and the air moans afar;
> *Le Matelot troublé, que son Art abandonne,*
> the troubled sailor whom his art forsakes,
> *Croit voir dans chaque Flot la Mort qui l'environne.*
> thinks he sees in each wave the Death that surrounds him.

4. "Cordage" refers to the conglomerate mass of ropes which comprise the rigging of a sailing ship.
5. A "Scotch mist" is a dense mist-like fine rain.
6. A "Herring-Hog" is a harbor porpoise (*Phocaena phocaena*).
7. "Hake" is any of several fishes constituting the genus *Merluccius* allied to the cods. The Silver Hake (*Merluccius bilinearis*) is common on the northern New England coast and is of importance as a food fish.
8. "Dog-fish" refers to any of various small sharks.
9. "Puncheons" are large casks of varying capacity but usually holding 70 imperial gallons.
10. "Hogsheads" are large casks or barrels usually containing 52½ imperial gallons.
11. "Muscovado Sugar" is unrefined or raw sugar obtained from the juice of the sugar cane by evaporation and drawing off the molasses.
12. "Snow-water" is water from melted snow.

THE
ARTS

My literary career began with the publication of *Zion's Friend*, a small annual paper of which I was the editor of the English department. For many years, my articles on Zionism appeared in *The Jewish Exponent* and *The Maccabean*.

When I came to Atlantic City, my writings, which heretofore had only occasionally been connected with my professional work, became more strictly confined to medicine, with particular emphasis on diseases of the eye and on medical history.

My first article following this pattern, entitled "Ophthalmology in the Bible and in the Talmud" (*Archives of Ophthalmology*, May 1933) was favorably received by my professional colleagues and by Semitic scholars. This encouraged me to continue writing a series of articles in various medical journals.

The favorable comments in the medical and lay press on my scattered articles inspired me to undertake a literary work of larger scope. Thus, I began to collect material for my book, The Romance of Medicine, which deals with the evolution of medicine from occult practices and primitive times, embracing folklore, customs, manners, traditions, and historical facts. This work appeared in 1944 and was reprinted in 1945. A second edition appeared in 1949, and a Spanish translation is pending.

Here again the very favorable reception given my work in the medical and lay press influenced me to write my most important and lengthy work, Medicine Throughout Antiquity (1949). This book received such cordial reviews that I am now working on a companion volume tentatively entitled, Medicine Throughout the Middle Ages and Renaissance.

Benjamin Lee Gordon, M.D.: Between Two Worlds: The Memoirs of a Physician. New York, 1952, pp. 331–335.

CHAPTER 8

*World of Music**

by

JONATHAN B. BAKER, A.B., LL.B.**

I. DIALECTS IN MUSIC

In spite of the familiar aphorism that music is a universal language, there are as many variations in performing the art as there are dialects within a language.

It is absolutely essential to be aware of these differences in order to avoid the error of criticizing a performer because his playing is in a style that is unfamiliar to us.

Although all nations have, to some extent, developed their own characteristic types of instrumental playing, the two most influential schools have been the French and the German.

The distinctions between them reflect something of the personalities of the two peoples.

The German bassoon, which has gained acceptance in all countries except France, has a smooth, throaty, mellow tone. The French style emphasizes a conspicuously brilliant reedy sound.

The French school of flute playing has been the dominant one in this century and continues to gain in importance. During the early twenties, the great flautists were Frenchmen who emigrated to the United States. They included, among others, Georges

---

*This chapter consists of a series of music appreciation articles published in *The Vancouver Sun* and *The Province* and is reprinted by permission of the publishers.

**Jonathan B. Baker, Esq. is the Director of The Community Music School of Greater Vancouver.

Barrere (New York Philharmonic) and Georges Laurent (Boston Symphony Orchestra).

Although there were stylistic variations, these phenomenal artists had in common an effervescent glittering tone, and since their students replaced them in positions of importance in American orchestras, we have come to expect from flautists this peculiarly French sonority.

The traditional German school is best represented by flautist Hubert Bahrwaser whose tone is dark and heavy. Whereas the French school features a light inconspicuous vibrato (the quaver or shake caused by varying the intensity of the breath), the German school features a wider and slower vibrato.

To some extent, the differences in tone are determined by modifications in construction of instruments. While the Germans prefer brass instruments of wide bore, the French instruments have a narrow bore, as for example the so called "pea shooter" trombone which has a strident, penetrating voice.

The difference in quality between the German bassoon developed by Heckel and the French instrument may be traced to acoustical variations, and to some extent this is also true of the oboe.

And while most flautists today use metal instruments of very light construction, both the Germans and English seem to prefer flutes with thicker metal tubing, and some even use the old wooden instruments.

It may happen that a particularly brilliant virtuoso may create his own school of playing. For example, Marcel Tabeteau, who was for years the solo oboist of the Philadelphia Orchestra, was considered by many to be the most influential woodwind player in America. Yet his heavily shaded non-nasal tone was neither typically French nor German.

As a result, there is an important school of oboe playing on this continent that may be traced to this exceptional artist.

On surveying the schools of instrumental playing, one observes that there is a growing tendency toward homogeneity that parallels political developments throughout the world.

European musicians travel and French musicians frequently appear with the Berlin Philharmonic while German musicians often perform with French orchestras.

II. THE ART OF CONDUCTING

What makes a great conductor? Is conducting an art related to choreography and dependent upon gracefulness of motion?

Does the conductor execute passages with his baton or does he rule the orchestra with it like a drill sergeant?

Is a brilliant performance entirely the result of rehearsals in which a conductor tells his musicians what he wants, or is it the result of some sort of magic of communication that happens on the stage at the live performance? Above all—what is the secret of genius in a conductor?

Some insights to these questions are provided in "The Conductor's Art," a collection of essays on conducting edited by Carl Bamberger.

The surprising thing about the articles, which include pieces by Leopold Stokowski, Richard Wagner, William Steinberg, Max Rudolf, Leonard Bernstein, and Eugene Ormandy among others, is that the authors are generally of the same mind on many aspects of the art.

All conductors seem to agree that the importance of conducting technique and beating time is minimal. It is of course essential to select the correct tempi (Wagner devotes an article exclusively to this subject) but the manner in which the stick is wielded is of no significance.

Steinberg is particularly outspoken in deploring the overemphasis of graceful technique, and says, "The clumsiest conductors . . . get marvelous results with whatever means are at their disposal, some of which they are completely unaware of . . . But from the so-called methodical conductors I have heard the most boring performances imaginable . . . Personality cannot be forced into a system."

Stokowski says on this matter, "Conducting is only to a small extent the beating of time—it is done far more through the eyes, still more it is done through a kind of inner communication between the players and the conductor."

Leonard Bernstein regards the essence of conducting as "the closest thing I know to love itself. On this current of love, the conductor can communicate at the deepest levels with his players, and ultimately with his audience."

Discussing technique, Bernstein emphasizes the importance of the upbeat. "The conductor always has to be at least a beat or two ahead of the orchestra. And he must hear two things at the same time . . . Therefore, the basic trick is the preparatory upbeat."

Bernstein's observations on this element of technique call to mind a story about Eugene Ormandy. Ormandy, regardless of what one thinks of his conducting, is not distinguished for the clarity of his beat.

The remarkable thing about it is that the sound of the orchestra never commences at the bottom of the downbeat but a split second thereafter.

A friend of mine, when he first joined the orchestra, had several mishaps when he anticipated his entrances by coming in on the bottom of the stroke. He was advised by a more experienced member that "you enter after the downbeat when the baton is on its way up and is opposite the third button on Mr. Ormandy's vest."

Max Rudolf's observations on the problems of the conductor in dealing with musicians are fascinating. All symphony members should bear in mind the following:

"Psychologists have noted that adults as members of a group develop juvenile traits, unfairness or even rudeness, which they would never permit themselves when acting as individuals.

"Thus the conduct of usually well-controlled and reasonable people can turn into mischievous classroom behavior if the leader of the group lacks authority. This problem does not exist for a conductor who knows how to maintain discipline without forgetting his sense of humor . . ."

All the work that leads to an inspired performance is not done in rehearsal. There seems to be agreement that the exceptional concert is the result of not only rehearsal time, but of the conductor's ability to communicate his ideas and feelings at the performance.

As to the secret of the conductor's genius—it should come as no surprise that even the greatest conductors seem unable to understand their own phenomenal abilities.

III. FROSTIANNA

Once every few months I check the latest Schwann Record Catalogue to see whether a work entitled "Frostianna" by Randall Thompson has been included among the new releases. I did so recently and once again found that it had not yet been recorded.

I saw the premier performance of this work at Amherst, Mass., in 1959. It was received rather cooly by the omniscient musicologists and critics who are legion in that part of the country, and nothing more was heard of it.

Six years might seem a long wait before writing a review, since most criticisms are written within moments of a performance, but something is to be said for allowing judgment to ripen. In addition, maybe this article can help retrieve "Frostianna" from oblivion.

Amherst, the home of Emily Dickinson, Ralph Waldo Emerson, and Robert Frost, was preparing for its bicentennial. There were to be parades, fairs, and even a poetry seminar on the works of Emily Dickinson in which Archibald Macleish would participate. But the major event was to be a performance of a choral work by Randall Thompson that had beeen commissioned by the town council and which was to put some of the poems of Robert Frost to music.

Some people had second thoughts about the choice of Thompson because Mr. Frost's conservative tastes in the arts were well known, and Mr. Thompson was no Stephen Foster. In more than one composition he had been guilty of departing from parallel thirds and fourths.

Frost on the other hand had hinted at some severe tests for art. For example, in paintings there should never be more than twice as many eyes as heads. His comment, "Too many eyes," upon viewing a considerably ocular modern painting at an exhibition, had not been forgotten. I suspect he would have agreed with Al Capp, who said of Jackson Pollock, "That's what happens when you don't teach a kid to clean up his messes."

"Frostianna" was performed by the Amherst College Glee Club and was conducted by the composer. It was said by several singers that Mr. Thompson, who had a warm respect for the poet, was most unnerved by his presence. If this was true, it was with good reason.

We all thought that this was going to be the most exciting event since Saint-Saens walked out on Stravinsky conducting his "Rites of Spring." Robert Frost was loved at Amherst not only for his poems but for his pranks, and there was much speculation about what the old man might do if he didn't like the work.

I sat across the aisle and about three rows behind Robert Frost at the performance and did not have to wait long for his reaction. Within minutes after the first piece began, Mr. Frost, a man capable of infinite degrees of subtlety, appeared to fall asleep.

The 85-year-old poet awoke shortly and was probably surprised by the traditionalism of Thompson. "Stopping by a Woods on a Snowy Evening" was ineffably lovely. To the lean, secularism of Frost's poems Thompson had added something of the quality of a Palestrina mass.

The finest work was the concluding one which I believe was entitled "Fix on Something Like a Star." He had done a reverent job, tampering little with Frost's phrasing, and had succeeded in translating the fragrance of poetry into music.

It is difficult to determine the poet's reaction. With the exception of the one piece which seemed to have a soporific effect, he politely applauded each selection. However, the rumors had it that he was unimpressed.

I don't know why nothing more has been heard of Randall Thompson's "Frostianna." If, however, the inanities of the critics had anything to do with it, I hope I can in part correct this injustice. "Frostianna" was a fine composition. Perhaps some choral group will attempt it locally sometime.

IV. CRITICAL BLUNDERS

Did Beethoven compose dull, ugly and vulgar music? Were the symphonies of Brahms aberrations into pure stupidity?

Readers who allow critics to influence their own judgment should be aware of what some of the most learned critics have said about the masters.

On hearing Beethoven's Second Symphony for the first time, a Vienna newspaper said it was "A crass monster, a hideously writhing, wounded dragon that refuses to expire, and though bleeding in the finale, furiously beats about with its tail erect."

The Third Symphony received the following review in the London Harmonican: "It contains much to admire but it is difficult to keep up admiration of this kind during three long quarters of an hour . . . If this symphony is not abridged, it will soon fall into disuse."

And the Seventh Symphony: "We cannot yet discover any design in it, neither can we trace any connection in its parts. Altogether it seem to have been intended as a kind of an enigma, we had almost said a hoax."—A London review.

If there is any work of Beethoven's that is almost worshipped it is the last movement from his Ninth Symphony. And yet Philip Hale, the noted Boston critic, was not mesmerized. On the contrary, he gave it the following review:

"But is not worship paid this symphony mere fetishism? Is not the famous scherzo insufferably long-winded: The finale is to me for the most part, dull and ugly . . . Oh, the pages of stupid and hopelessly vulgar music! The unspeakable cheapness of the chief tune, 'Freude, Freude.' Do you believe in the bottom of your heart that if this music had been written by John L. Tarbox, now living in Sandom, New Hampshire, any conductor here or in Europe could be persuaded to put it in rehearsal."

George Bernard Shaw is commonly regarded as a great music critic. Of Brahms he said, ". . . a commonplace mind." His music had "nothing better in the way of ideas to express than incoherent commonplace . . . aberrations into pure stupidity!"

"There are some sacrifices which should not be demanded twice from any man; and one of them is listening to Brahm's Requiem. On some future evening, perhaps when the weather is balmy, and I can be accommodated with a comfortable armchair, an interesting book, and all the evening newspapers, I may venture; but last week I should have required a requiem for myself if I had attempted such a feat of endurance. I am sorry to have to play the 'disgruntled' critic over a composition so learnedly contrapuntal, not to say fugacious; but I really cannot stand Brahms as a serious composer."

Tastes in music are not derived from universal truths. A person could well believe that Mozart's "Jupiter Symphony" is but the cooings of an idiot compared to a Bartok string quartet or that Stravinsky's "Rites of Spring" is an obscenity compared to Brahms at his worst. But the correctness of such judgments is no more demonstrable than the correctness of a preference of rye for gin.

V. WORDS TO LISTEN BY

I have always belonged to the Cult of the Mute Response to Music. That is to say I believe in most cases it is better not to talk about music.

Although I violate the principles of the cult every time I write a piece of criticism, I nevertheless think that most of what is written on music contributes nothing to a listener's appreciation and may actually serve to confuse him.

*   *   *

A music appreciation book has now been written that attempts to undo all the damage that has been done to music by critics and musicologists.

"This is Music" by David Randolph (Mentor, 75 cents) develops the idea also set forth in Leonard Bernstein's "The Joy of Music" that music stands on its own.

There is no need for the listener to be aware of the names of harmonic relationships or to be told that the opening phrases of Beethoven's Fifth represent fate knocking at the door.

The sort of writing Randolph condemns is that which is commonly found in program notes. It is the profoundly dull explanation that says something like, "the theme begins in the key of C Major at which point it proceeds upward an octave and one half and downwards two octaves, accompanied by sforzando in the strings."

The reader who has no formal background in music will read this sort of nonsense at a concert. It sounds terribly wise to him and since he doesn't really know what it is all about, he develops a musical inferiority complex.

Randolph quotes George Bernard Shaw who demonstrated how unrelated such purely technical analyses are to any real appreciation of music. Applying the typical music commentator's method to Hamlet's soliloquy "To be or not to be," Shaw wrote:

"Shakespeare, dispensing with the customary exordium, announces his subject at once in the infinitive, in which mood it is presently repeated after a short connecting passage in which, brief as it is, we recognize the alternative and negative forms on which so much of the significance of repetition depends. Here we reach a colon: and a pointed pository phrase, in which the accent falls decisively on the relative pronoun, bringing us to the first full stop."

The second kind of futile analysis of music consists of ascribing extra meaning to music.

A perfect example of this can be found on the record jacket for a Norwegian recording of Grieg that was recently released. The music, says the jacket scribe, is "redolent of Norway's pines." How can an orchestra sound like a pine tree?

This is the kind of writing that seeks to attach meaning to every note in a composition. A minor key in Beethoven's Third is said to represent clouds passing over the sun, or Napoleon's misbehaviour, or something equally remote from music.

Randolph points out that both absolute music and program music are the same in this one respect. Neither are representational. Music can, according to certain conventions, represent vague moods.

*   *   *

It can be animated and playful, or slow and comtemplative and so forth but it can not represent an ocean, a sky, or fate knocking at a door. The opening themes of Victory at Sea, for example, have nothing uniquely nautical about them. The melody seems to have a rolling motion but it could represent hills, mountains, or the excitement of two armies preparing to clash.

The objection Randolph has to an emphasis on the program notes is that it distracts the listener from really enjoying the music.

VI. PROGRAM NOTES

Performers who are presented by the Friends of Chamber Music are always at a disadvantage because no matter how brilliant their playing, they can only approach the ineffable beauty of the program notes.

In terms of sheer linguistic grandeur, program notes are perhaps the most overpowering literary form. They bridge the gap between language and music.

Last night, the Friends of Chamber Music presented the Trio di Trieste at the Queen Elizabeth Theatre. The first work performed was Haydn's "Trio No. 4 in E Major."

The program notes describe the work as follows: "The Fourth Trio in E begins with a lyrical melody accompanied by a staccato bass. Its restatement is embellished with chromatic passing notes giving a touch of romantic color."

In those lusty words is there not the quintessence of Haydn? One can not read this passage without being moved.

The Trio, which consisted of a violin, cello, and piano, performed the work well enough for they are virtuosos. But no degree of virtuosity can possibly sustain our feverish feelings when the performers actually arrive at "the lyrical melody accompanied by a staccato bass." The beauty of the language transcends that of the music.

But if the notes for Haydn were impassioned, those for Ravel's "Trio in A Minor" (1914) were orgiastic. One's eyes became glazed at the delicious words . . . "the third movement is a free passacaglia in which the theme, instead of remaining as a ground bass, moves into a higher register accompanied by an increasingly amplified texture."

In this passage the writer has captured the Bacchanalian revelry that is found in Ravel. There is no need to sit through 20 minutes of unfamiliar and unwanted music when such notes are available.

The final work to be read and which was also performed was Beethoven's "Trio in B Flat Major, Opus 97." Of that piece it was said, "Just before the recapitulation, the strings resume arco. The subject matter is now treated very differently from the layout in the exposition. A short coda in which the piano part is amplified and quickened by semiquavers brings the movement to its final climax and conclusion."

Does the music of Beethoven ever reach these dizzy heights of passion? Here is the distillation of all that the composer has ever expressed, beginning in ethereal wonder and ending in transcendent joy.

VII. PATRIOTIC SONGS

Now, at last, the war in Viet Nam has produced a patriotic song. (There have been plenty of unpatriotic ones.) The composer of this masterpiece is Dr. ——— ———, a Philadelphia dentist.

A recent newspaper article conveys the information that Dr. ——— "drills teeth by day and concocts new rhythms on his violin at night." Inspiration for his efforts, the article says, comes from Abraham Lincoln and his own mother.

The following are some of the lyrics to "We've Got a Job to do in Viet Nam":
"We knocked the 'L' out of Hitler for an Allied victory."
"We'll knock the 'O' out of Viet Cong and keep Viet Nam free."

It may be that "We've Got a Job to do in Viet Nam" will live on like "The Battle Hymn of the Republic," but I somehow doubt it.

For those musicologists who are interested in other works by the author, the same article advises that he has written, "We're the Guys—GIs who'll win the war" and another Korean War song, "We Yanks Will Give You Hell Past the 38th Parallel."

Because of the meteoric obscurity he has achieved in his lifetime, it seems to me that the life of Dr. ——— would be an ideal doctoral thesis for some Ph.D. candidate and I hope that some enterprising scholar takes advantage of this lead.

VIII. LA SCALA'S LA BOHEME

It is ironic that a mediocre movie can run for months in Vancouver but a truly magnificent production, as was the La Scala version of La Boheme, shown at the Orpheum Wednesday night will be here for only two more performances.

This Warner Brothers production is the second version of Puccini's opera that has been filmed. I had the opportunity to see the first, a German production, in Philadelphia more than five years ago. It had much to recommend it musically, but it also contained those aggravations that are bound to produce allergies to opera among those who love both drama and music.

When the German Mimi extended her great arms lovingly towards the camera they looked like two giant bolognas in loose casings. And when Musetta, a famous Wagnerian soprano, semaphored her emotions as she lumbered about the set, it was like an old Daimler-Benz signalling a left.

She entered the set with the grace of a lobster trying to back into a bottle. When she breathed it was as vociferous as a vacuum cleaner.

Attending the La Scala version of La Boheme and expecting the usual difficulties of opera would be intensified on film, I was ready as critic to ambush the first battalion of fat belledames who rumbled onto the set.

From the first brief shot of the great Herbert Von Karajan directing the La Scala Orchestra it was clear that this would be no ordinary production.

The opening scene of the opera takes place in a bohemian garret in Paris. Rudolph, a writer, and Marcel, an artist, are trying to work.

Having exhausted their fuel they debate as to which piece of furniture or art should be sacrificed for a fire and settle on Rudolph's latest manuscript. Shortly Schaunard, a philosopher, and Colline, a musician, enter. Colline has sold a composition.

Deciding that a celebration is in order all save Rudolph head for the nearest pub.

While Rudolph is working, Mimi, the soprano upstairs, comes down, loses her key, and before long Rudolph has her hand in his and sings "How Cold is your Little Hand." The ploy works and the scene concludes with a declaration of their love.

Meanwhile at the pub Marcel meets his love, Musetta, a voluptuous blonde. The opera deals with the love stories of Mimi and Rudolph as well as Marcel and Musetta.

In every aspect La Boheme is superb. Mimi (Mme. Freni) and Musetta are both beautiful and have glorious voices. The male leads are excellent.

What is more unusual in opera, however, is that the acting was brilliant. There were no horrific grimaces or other torturous behavior which so often is a characteristic of opera.

Camera techniques were orthodox and restrained. There were no trick shots from helicopters but there were closeups.

In order to avoid the possibly unpleasant sight of Mme. Freni with her mouth wide open and her tonsils exposed in such shots, the sound was dubbed and she merely smiled in time to the music.

Whether or not the reader is an opera lover, this film is urged. If you see it and still don't like Boheme your opera allergy is incurable.

IX. MUSIC AND THE ARMY

About three weeks ago, my last pair of army socks wore out. They had lasted a little less than two years for it has been that long this Christmas since I completed my six months of active duty with the U.S. Army at Fort Ord, California.

I spent my four months after basic training with the Post Army Band and my final rehearsal with that organization came just before Christmas of 1963.

The conductor was appointed to his position about the same time that I and 29 others had been shifted to the band. A Negro from the slums of Newark, New Jersey, his ambition to become a paratrooper was thwarted when he quite innocently mentioned on one of the army questionnaires that he had been a rock and roll drummer in high school.

Instead of joining the airborne, he suddenly found that he had been made kapellmeister of one of McNamara's bands.

At our first rehearsal, he informed the band while it respectfully stood at ease that he could not read music and had little experience listening to the sort of things that an army band was expected to play. However, he assured us that he would "utilize his abilities" and do the best he could.

The first step the novice conductor took was to assess our musical resources. It soon became apparent that he was not the only member of the band with limited musical experience. Of the 30 new members, at least 20 were cymbal players. Having realized that there were advantages in being in a band instead of the infantry, these boys had successfully requested duties as cymbalists.

It was ordered that those who could play were to instruct the cymbal players how to double on other instruments. I became a flute instructor.

The first score that was handed out was the background music for "Terrytoon" cartoons. This was followed by the Pathetique

Symphony which our conductor informed us he had once heard on his car radio.

He requested that only those who knew how to play should do so. To his amazement, he found that once a beat was established, he could lead us through the first movement of Tchaikovsky.

The first rehearsal left him euphoric. He might not have wanted to be a bandsman to start with, but if the army put him there he had every intention of becoming a conductor. And so day and night he worked at learning how to read music and becoming familiar with the classics.

Fortunately, he was assisted in these matters by a brilliant Hungarian concert pianist who was serving as a cook in a neighboring company.

Meanwhile, I was having mixed results with my students. The most promising one was a 19-year-old boy from Nebraska who had enlisted because he was told that he would receive training useful to his profession. (He was a crop duster.)

The final rehearsal that I had with the band was shortly before Christmas.

By then, our conductor not only could read scores but was directing with sensitivity band arrangements of Schubert symphonies and Rossini overtures which he had grown to love. He had become a conductor.

My Nebraskan student had become a flautist which, he concluded after reading Rachael Carson's "Silent Spring," could do little damage to wildlife.

In fact, the only person who was unhappy that Christmas was the Hungarian pianist. It was said that he was a terrible cook.

My mother often called for me at the House of Study
when I did not return home at a reasonable hour. She
frequently found me alone, standing in front of a high
and narrow desk with a candle in my right hand and a
large worm-eaten volume in front of me, absorbed in a
certain topic and like as not humming some sad tune. I
can well remember how the sudden appearance of my
mother emerging from the shadows into the candlelight
used to startle me. Frequently I felt tears running down
my cheeks, but I could not explain the cause of this.

Surely my studies were usually not concerned with sad
topics. Often I was engrossed in dry legal matters such
as for example, *"shor shenagah et hapara"* (the laws invoked when an ox gores a cow) or *"getz sheyyatsa mithat
hapatish"* (the laws invoked when a spark of a hammer
sets fire to a load of hay)—subjects which were nothing
to cry about. My mother often asked what ailed me, but
I did not know what to answer her.

Since I could write, I always tried to put things down
on paper that I could not express orally, and sometimes I
tried to do this in rhyme. In answer to my mother's question I wrote a number of rhymes in Yiddish. The first
stanza of one I later translated into English as follows:

> Why do I weep,
> Why do I cry?
> It lies so deep
> I know not why.

Benjamin Lee Gordon, M.D.: Between Two Worlds: The Memoirs
of a Physician. New York, 1952, pp. 59–60.

CHAPTER 9

Poems

by

SUSAN JOAN GORDON, M.D.*

VARSHAVA

Subterranean world
Dank with mildew, rotting with inconsequential history
Well-worn paths
Crying with blood-stained experience, damp with the self-
   same tears
That burn the flesh of my face
I cannot remember how it is that I am here
Chronological inversion
My soul
My key to long-locked gates must be somewhere within this lost
   and dusty world
Choking with asthmatic wheeze
I am searching
Searching
Have been searching
Through irrelevant millennia
For what?
Perhaps, in the darkness, I have stumbled upon Cabalah

---

* Susan Joan Gordon, M.D., is a gastroenterologist and member of the faculty of Jefferson Medical College. She is the author of a book of poems, "The Road I Travel."

In the desperation
Too early
And am now irrevocably doomed
Even by the search itself
Knowledge
The infinite destruction
Suddenly I see
Or think I see
Through eye or delusion
Lightless photons in the blackness
Ethereal boundary to an endless world
On the underside of earth
Beyond the Styx
I see!
Perhaps it is occipital, bypassing stimulation of the retina
The river-sea without end
And yet—
Could this be?
A raft
Boatman!
I know you!
Solemn Zur-Shanabi
Can it be this which I have sought
In vain and worthless endeavor?
Noiselessly gliding over black water
Glassy rent without wave
If I go to death, at least free of pain
The endless etiological searching
The air is cold and damp
Emotionless
The oarsman is silent
I try to offer some communication
But the air is too dense to be cut by words I cannot say
Sounds I do not know how to make
Without comfort
And yet the desperation seems eased
And pain is less
In reality or fantasy
The opposite shore exists

Is approached
And somehow—
Without reason—
The same as the shore departed
Nothing is here
I disembark
Afraid, as always
And suddenly feel the need to breech the chasm to the
  known world
To touch the hand of the oarsman
But cannot
He goes
I see you now
Although there is nothing detectable by any sense I know
I feel your whole long tenure of life
I want to be as you were
I want the strength
The vision
The wisdom
The power
Totality of you
I cannot speak to tell you
Only a lacrimal veil between us
You are my life
My thought
My love
The end
And I
But a milkweed weeping bitter white tears for the torn leaf
The time was infinitesimally small
No word
No touch
And yet
Since I have returned from the forbidden shore
Through the catacombs to light
From the place I cannot be sure I have seen
In life
Or in a dream
I know

It is you
The end is you
It must be the constant, unbroken line from the beginning of
    organic life
Deoxyribose
Adenine, thymine
Cytosine, guanine
Mutated
But you
And I am you among the living
And what there is
Shall be
Because of you
Because you loved me

A VIGNETTE
(*to Margaret*)

Softly calls the wind
Whispering across the winter-grey sea
Endlessly, endlessly has it blown
This way
And always, as before,
In the time when the plesiosaur
Lived where I do now
In a place dimensionless of time
Where Sumerian could not impose
The sixty-sixty-sixty
That makes us history
And binds us to mortality
And so he is immortal
Come, my friend. You have the power, I know
Since the hour-god stays you not
Take me, take me there
Where once I stood on the summer sand
A child
No, not the memorable day—
The day forgotten—
Where there she stands
In the ocher light
Young, it seems; alive—so alive—and always
That part of me which is the wind
And the sky
And the quiescent sea
Free from periodicity
She is there when the sea gull skims the frothy wave
And when the ghost crab skitters by my hand
Disappearing into the tiny abyss
And when I find a brittle starfish
Or discover the secret of the conch's egg case
Or stumble over the odd romantic remains
Of a horseshoe crab
To muse over its five hundred million year past

And wonder why it alone should remain
Of the trilobites
She is there
It was she who gave me the ribbon to tie my waistlength hair
It was she who made me the sweater which I wore on the
     summer's night
It was she who gave her soul to me for a birthright
To be as her heir, yet I could not be of the form that she was
For all the vital breath she bestowed
She demanded not that I be she
But only asked the right to love
The quiet little scion with the flaxen hair matted with sand
Standing ankle deep in the summer sea
The day is so warm, so bright
It is more real than the frozen winter which I left
To stand on the burning sand with her whom I love
Oh wait, restless wind, linger yet a moment
While she brushes back the vagrant strands
Of straw-white hair with bony caress
Oh, soft infinity, the time is gone with you
And I
Stand alone before the winter sea
Here she is sad and wasted, the clinging root sentimentality
Nourishing the yellow curled remains of the leaves of life
Was it that the omnipotent farmer endlessly plowing the rows
Cast on her too great a burden
Too many thirsting leaves to feed from one root—
Or was it that I was so young?
And yet for all that was
And is
Though nothing more seems yet to be
Save for the wind, the softly calling wind
The endlessly blowing wind
Whispering across the sea
I love her yet the more

THOUGHTS WHILE LISTENING TO
A BARBER SONATA

Whispers
grey
the summer's day
softly springs
on ibis wings

Laughter
white
the summer's night
reluctant grieves
sumac leaves

A SUMMER STORY IN TWO CHAPTERS
(to my father, who shared it)

My hope was shattered two years ago
As I stood gazing wondrously
  into the secret orderly world of a tiny bird sanctuary.
The ancient summer-green trees were heavy
  with their burden of magnificent egrets,
  And the brush beneath was thick with whimbrels.
Everything was in its place:
The whimbrels made no attempt to invade
  the lofty perch of the egrets,
  And the egrets condescendingly allotted
  the ground to the whimbrels,
And would not occupy that place
  though the trees were so full,
  So crowded with graceful, large white life
  that the branches bent beneath the weight.
It was then that a young glossy ibis circled the area,
  Scouting a place for his tired body.
He landed, at last, off to the side
  on a barren, leafless branch
  vacant of life.
He made no attempt to dislodge another bird,
  Only to rest wearily on his lifeless branch
  in peace.
But, hapless creature! he had disturbed the status quo,
  That magical quantity that limits all of man's endeavors.
  It tears my soul to know
  that a status quo
  should limit nature too.
How can we overcome it all—
  that most major of our shortcomings—
  If they will not set us the example?
Five of the largest, most lordly egrets
  (apparently assigned to such tasks)

beset the tiny intruder,
   Driving him from his branch
   and from the sanctuary.
There was no place for the dark little bird
   in this haven for large white birds
   (though except for this they were the same).
The order of society had not left him a place.
My heart ached for two years
   but my pen was inarticulate,
   For fear of feeding the fires of hate
   which consume men who say,
   "God made us different and separate.
   Nature is against it."
But now the story is finished
   and I must tell it all.
Long, long months later, today,
   I travelled to a remarkable place:
   A sanctuary unhampered by lack of space,
Where egrets and gulls, with black-crowned night herons
   roam the summer expanse freely
   In haphazard array
   unpressed by fences.
The disorder of the nature of things,
   the lack of a hierarchy,
   Pleased my being immeasurably.
As I left, a sight met my eye
   which seemed so natural
   I barely noticed.
My eye mechanically recorded its occurrence
   While it took my lacadaisical brain
   many hours to comprehend its significance:
A young egret, as white and as lovely as any,
   was feeding by the side of a glossy ibis
   of exactly the same size,
Freely, happily, sociably, on the same sandbar
   Sharing their quota of fiddler crabs.
This I saw.
At first it was only beautiful
   and I enjoyed the sight of it.

Now I wonder if the eyes of Joseph
    might have seen in it a proverb.
Now it seems to me that this is the answer:
In a very large sanctuary
    unhampered by fences
If the two are really of equal stature
Peace is possible.

PYRGIAN ONE

For one who braved the coral spikes
relentless starfish eating reef
the crown of thorns digesting all
who yet failed not to also see
deep within the flaming tree
the purple sea anemone

That knew the dank and musty cave
that fostered rabid bats
salamanders without eyes
could nurture in its hidden core
mysterious chronologic door
timeless niche for plesiosaur

He who wallowed in quicksand marsh
with stench of rotting ferns and leaves
and hydrogen sulfide gas
to acknowledge one prophetic hour
living in a putrid tower
sweet clandestine mallow flower

To him among the dying goes
transcience and fear
hideous to all
yet knows that in his gentle hand
in port however contraband
a boat to Sheol for mortal man

Who knows within a compost heap
a morning-glory lives
and soon will die
but life would come then life would wane
and all of life would be in vain
but for him who bore the pain

He who sought among the flocks
of barnyard fowl
of albatross
he from all who stood alone
perceived the vision long unknown
and spent his tears for the cygnet grown

CHAPTER 10

Metamorphoses

WOODCUTS, SCULPTURES AND DRAWINGS

by

DEBORAH J. GORDON, A.B.

Photograph of Original Sculpture by Deborah J. Gordon

Photograph of Original Sculpture by Deborah J. Gordon

Photograph of Original Sculpture by Deborah J. Gordon

Photograph of Original Sculpture by Deborah J. Gordon

Photograph of Original Sculpture by Deborah J. Gordon

Photograph of Original Sculpture by Deborah J. Gordon

Photograph of Original Sculpture by Deborah J. Gordon

Photograph of Original Sculpture by Deborah J. Gordon

Portrait in Brown Conte by Deborah J. Gordon

Still Life Etching by Deborah J. Gordon

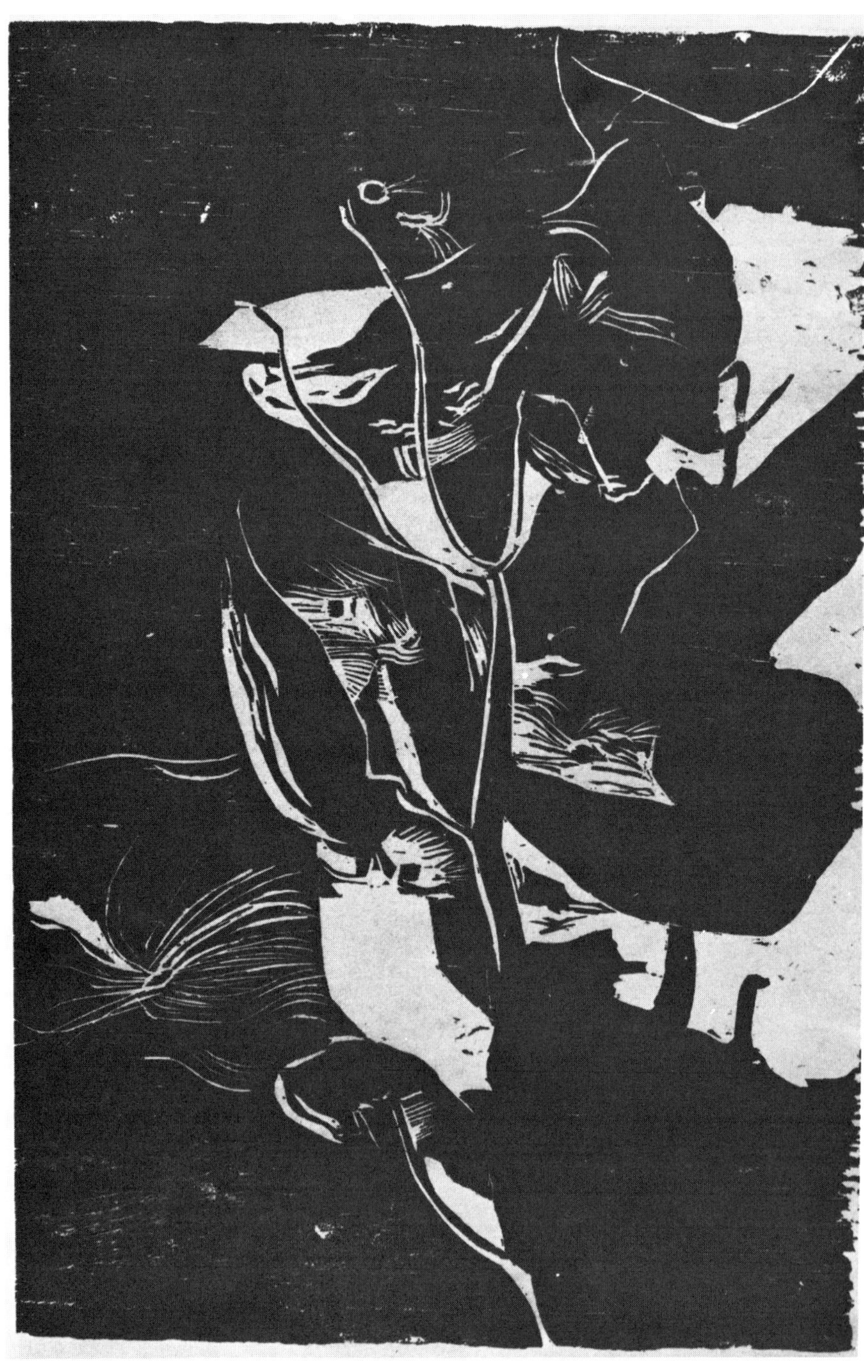

Woodcut: Study of Milkweed by Deborah J. Gordon

Still Life Woodcut by Deborah J. Gordon

Woodcut Portrait by Deborah J. Gordon

Woodcut from an Original Sculpture by Deborah J. Gordon

Portrait in Charcoal by Deborah L. Gordon

CHAPTER 11

Three Untitled Poems

by

SARAH YAEL GORDON*

UNTITLED 1

Kingdom (willed) of the Unsaid,
in deepest regal passion draped,
you, without the mockery
of taming words, assurances
(majesty and silence-stripp'd),
have seized the root of lovers' blood:
you cast your grasp into the heart,
the other heart, and back again.

To decorate the lovers' bed
you never leave a single shade,
so no betrayals of the night
and no denials need be made.

And yet you know they welcome you
with nodless, voiceless greeting spil't;
no loss will ever mark the womb,
no life will end where you have dwelt.

---

*Sarah Yael Gordon is an undergraduate student in Theater Arts at Brandeis University.

UNTITLED 2

The seasons show no commitment in their coming,
so as not to be held to anything.
No commitment
but a promise
to have been.
They loosen up they fade they edge over they edge off.
lingering leaving leaves
lingering

Spring has come in hours of transport
reserving the right to be playing,
sudden
with vagrant rain undoing
what has been done
by way of change
to time.

UNTITLED 3

When, in reconstituted game,
big people join their hands and sing
of life refound, of child reborn
in threatless, joyous playfulness;
when, in reconstituted game,
big peephole in the joiner's hands
shows life reflex and child reworn
in threadless, joyless play fullness,
Child's Young Sweet Song is not resung,
and only death has been begun.
I don't advise a childish shout
in answer to the inside-out,
but hear, beyond the inside in,
a footstep

where the child has been.